"The Shape of Things" Neil Labute

• Kate Chopin "The Awakening"

"The Ghost of Mrs. Muir" "camille" "All about Eve"

A DOLL'S HOUSE

"Stardust"

A PLAY IN THREE ACTS

By HENRIK IBSEN

TRANSLATED BY
WILLIAM ARCHER

WITH A BIOGRAPHICAL AND CRITICAL INTRODUCTION

PREPARED FOR THE PRESENT EDITION BY
EDMUND GOSSE

Copyright, 1890, by JOHN W. LOVELL CO.

BOSTON
WALTER H. BAKER & CO.

D0124912

HENRIK IBSEN.

INTRODUCTION.

In presenting to the American public the first collected
version of the works of Ibsen, it may not be uninterest-
ing to consider in what particulars the local position of
his genius, and the society out of which it springs, present a similarity with those out of which the great
American dramatist, that phœnix of the future, will
have to struggle to the sun. Norway, like America, but
like no other country of the modern world—since the
republics of South America can scarcely boast the same
conditions—is a young and a vigorous people, which has
broken away from an ancient power, whose population
it now greatly outnumbers. In each case the parent,
instead of dwindling in intellectual vitality after the se-
cession, has rather increased in vigor and individuality;
while, although developing a public spirit entirely inde-
pendent, the child has preserved the paternal traditions
of the race on most essential points. And more than
all besides, through each political and social schism the
language has remained the same, as an inseparable bond
of unity. As, therefore, in considering a great American talent, we are obliged to look back and see what
roots it has sent down into the earth of English litera-

ture, so, to conceive arightly how a genius like Ibsen's has become what it is, we must briefly see what it owes to its Danish as well as its Norwegian predecessors.

When Henrik Ibsen was a very young man, when he first appeared before the public as the author of that crude Roman tragedy " *Catalina,* " Norwegian literature, as a separate growth, was still in its boyhood. The hot, romantic lyrics of Wergeland were its most characteristic products. In drama it had practically done nothing. The Norwegian poet who desired to write for the stage —and Ibsen has been essentially a dramatist from his earliest lispings—was obliged to look to Denmark for his inspiration. In that energetic little country he would find, forty years ago, a condition of things calculated to dazzle the judgment of a provincial. Copenhagen, from 1805 to 1845, was perhaps the country in the world in which dramatic literature flourished best and was the most judiciously fostered. During the greater part of that time the severe and beautiful genius of Adam Oehlenschläger was filling the stage with his stately figures, creating a national and historical body of tragic poetry so pure, and, in its earlier forms at least, so exquisite and tender, that, whatever is neglected, young men and maidens in Scandinavia must always read Oehlenschläger as they must read Walter Scott with us. When the influence of Oehlenschläger's tragedies was on the wane, a school of refined poetical comedy began to assert itself in Copenhagen, with, at its head, Henrik Hertz, in my judgment not one of the strongest, indeed, but one of the most exquisite poets that the nineteenth century has produced in Europe. The famous translation of Shakespeare by Foersom was the direct model upon which these Danish writers of romantic comedy proceeded. Their whole outlook upon life was fanciful and optimistic, or else national and heroic, in either case purely romantic; and this dramatic serenity was only broken by occasional fits of local or temporary satire, mere outbreaks of stage petulance at the creaking of the times.

In order to understand Ibsen, whose figure has been too often presented to us of late as though it were a perfectly solitary one, we must try to realize the apothecary's apprentice of 1848 in his little, miserable shop at Grimstad, looking, in all his ignorance and *ennui*, toward a distant and magnificent Copenhagen, in which, at the King's Theatre, mighty figures of buskined actors and superb actresses with sweeping trains were spouting the resonant iambics of Oehlenschläger, or delicately emphasizing the points of the rhyming couplets of Hertz.* In " *Catalina* " we seem to see the work of an ambitious lad who has read nothing but Foersom's Shakespeare and a few tragedies of Oehlenschläger; and it is very important to see this great realist starting from the innermost recesses of romanticism. But the change was not to be only in Ibsen; it moved in all Scandinavian drama also. It was in 1849, the year in which Ibsen completed his " *Catalina* " in Norway, that J. L. Heiberg became sole director of the Royal Theatre at Copenhagen, and by his cynical wit and satire, by his recognition of the requirements of the modern audience, and by his encouragement of a more realistic and less merely " po-

* I do not know that any writer has noted the influence of Hertz's "Amors Genistreger" (1839) upon the form of Ibsen's "Love's Comedy."

etical " drama, did more than any other man to prepare
for the Scandinavian theatre of to-day.

The career of Ibsen, happily not yet completed nor
even past its prime, has of late been so often chronicled
that it is not needful to dwell upon it here in detail.
For the first twenty years of his work for the stage he
remained strictly in the Scandinavian ideal. His four
tragedies of Norwegian history, published from 1856 to
1864, form the earliest of these sections of his work.
They possess a certain severity of form which is characteristic of their author, and they are written in the
plainest prose, instead of blank verse ; but they are
nevertheless wholly romantic in character, and not to be
distinguished, in kind, from what other poets were doing
at the same time. Not one of them perhaps is quite
equal to Björnson's " *Sigurd Slembe.*" In 1863 Ibsen
began to occupy an entirely fresh field. Retaining in a
measure the sublyrical forms adopted by Hertz and his
school in Denmark, he turned the artillery of his delicate rhymes and flowing epigrammatic verse against the
follies, narrowness, and weaknesses of local Norwegian
society. "Love's Comedy " forms the brightest and
lightest expression of this particular class of his genius.
The manner deepened into the gloom of " *Brand*" and
widened into the lambent wit, splendid and whimsical
fancy, and penetrating insight of " *Peer Gynt.*" These
poems have been described as forming a trilogy of sa-
tiric drama, but they resemble one another more in
form than in anything else. The singularity is that all
three were written in running rhymed verse, and in the
cases of " *Brand* " and " *Peer Gynt* " in verse of a kind
so rapid, brief, and profuse, and so absolutely unflagging,

that not Goethe himself has bequeathed to the world a dramatic *tour de force* more amazing.

It would be exceedingly pleasant to dwell on the characteristics of these picturesque and highly original, if imperfect, poems. In another place I have attempted to analyze their contents, and to give some specimens of what any translator may despair of reproducing at length—their sententious melody and richness. But fine as these rhymed dramas are, and firmly as a poet of less ambition might be willing to base his reputation upon them, they form but an episode in Ibsen's dramatic career. There are not wanting signs, to those who are familiar with his early work, that he was already dissatisfied with the ideals of his youth and was preparing for a crisis in style. One of the characters in his "*Warriors at Helgeland*," had said, "Sing! no, I could do that yesterday ; to-day I am too old." It seemed as though Ibsen almost suddenly grew too old, too serious, for the gentle agitation of prosody ; as though in the very maze of the linked melodies of "*Peer Gynt*" he had whispered to himself, "these indictments are too serious, these charges too heavy and too direct, to be accompanied by a tinkling of the lyre." In the fourth act of that poem he had said things almost too scathing, too bitter to be said in verse. Such accusations against humanity ought to be made in prose or not made at all. So he seems to have reflected, and suddenly a new form of dramatic art occurred to him as that for the execution of which he had naturally been born into the world.

This first experiment in it was a little conventional, and at all events deserved no particular attention through its novelty of form. The zealous Ibsenites of to-day have almost forgotten " *The Young Men's League* " (De Unges Forbund) of 1869, but it is really the first of the master's social dramas, and should take its place in every list of them. More than this, although shorn of all the lyrical beauties of his preceding writings, it showed a very great advance in intellectual power. Those who have read Ibsen's saga-dramas and rhymed plays must have been struck with the part which abstract ideas, personations of virtues and vices, rather than real human beings, had occupied in his thoughts. His conceptions were apt to be symbolic ; even " *Brand* " in his pathetic and solitary sacrifice, even " *Peer Gynt* " as he wallows in the sensual sty, are but human beings now and then, and, as a rule, are shadows cast by the poet's genius in his reflection. It was first in " *The Young Men's League* " that Ibsen stood with his feet firmly pressed to earth, and this great gain in character-painting may well overbalance the occasional dryness and poorness of this prose comedy. There is, moreover, no longer that element of vague locality, that tract of fairyland, which had marked Ibsen's earlier pieces, which marks even " *Love's Comedy* " in spite of the attempt there to be strictly realistic.

It could not perhaps be said that the spirit of the poet himself was first plainly seen in an awakened condition of unrest in this drama. The author of " *Brand* " had scarcely been at peace with existing conditions of society, nor the author of " *Peer Gynt* " an optimist. He had already been in a mood to say, in the famous words of Sören Kierkegaard : " the passion of my soul is scorn ; " but it is in this comparatively mild piece that we first detect the germs of Ibsen's peculiar attitude toward social questions, his bitter democracy, his policy of " root and branch." But, as a matter of fact, "*The Young Men's League*" is tentative, slightly imitative of ancient Danish phases of satirical drama, and with little of the peculiar inward flame which is to his real admirers the peculiar attraction of Ibsen's work. The play, moreover, is so locally and exclusively Norwegian that it almost needs a commentary to explain it to Anglo-Saxon readers. The central character in it, the political adventurer Stensgaard, is the born brother of Bernick in the "*Pillars of Society*," a respectable scoundrel of the true Ibsen type. But in the circumstances of his intrigues, and in particular in the fact that he makes love to three women at one time, we see Ibsen relying a little on the old Holberg tradition of Danish comedy, and working it rather heavily. In the character of Selma he breaks away from the Danish ideal, and gives us a sketch or silhouette of one of that piquant and individualized family of women, of whom Nora and Rebecca and Mrs. Alving are the most famous sisters. "I cannot hold silence and be a hypocrite and a liar any longer," says Selma, in the middle of the third act, and we have hopes of her ; but therefrom she fades into a mere phantom in the piece, and scarcely ever speaks in the last two acts.

From 1869, the year of the production of "*The Young Men's League*," to 1877, when "*The Pillars of Society*" appeared, Ibsen was going through a very curious crisis. He began to take his literary analysis and his moral curiosity very "hard." He lost his last shred of confidence in literature as an anodyne, and he became a more zealous enemy of æsthetic and formal beauty in poetry than those who had never been adepts in teaching "the tender stops of various quills." He took farewell of

verse in his collected volume of lyrics in 1870, a review
of which, from the pen of the present writer, was the
first introduction of his name to an English audience, and
the origin of a personal friendship which is now nearing
its twentieth year. He rejected verse as a vehicle before
he saw his way to the abandonment of all those themes
of which verse is the natural ornament. His only work
of importance during these eight years was the historical
play " *Keiser og Galilœar* " (Emperor and Galilean), a
vast, ten-act tragedy—as long as Dryden's " *Conquest of
Granada* "—on the career of Julian the Apostate. This
curious book was written in prose, and marks the transi-
tion. Ibsen had " grown weary of his long-loved mis-
tress, Rhyme," and from that day to this he has used it
only in short copies of verses. The announcement of his
complete divorce reached me in a letter from which I
will here translate a few words. He had told me of the
preparation he was making for a new play—the same
which afterward appeared as " *Samfundet's Stötter* "—
and I ventured, with plentiful lack of judgment, as
the event proved, to beg that it might be in verse. Dr.
Ibsen replied :

"There is one point which I must discuss with you.
You think my new drama ought to be written in verse,
and that it will gain an advantage if it is. Here I must
simply contradict you ; for the piece is, as you will find,
developed in the most realistic way possible. The illu-
sion I wish to produce is that of truth itself ; I want to
produce upon the reader the impression that what he is
reading is actually taking place before him. If I were
to use verse, I should by so doing be stultifying my own
intention and the object which I placed before me. The

variety of every-day and unimportant characters which I
have intentionally introduced into the piece, would be
effaced (udviskede) and blended into one another if I
had allowed them all to converse in a rhythmic move-
ment. We are no longer living in the time of Shakespeare, and among sculptors there is beginning to be a
discussion whether statuary ought not to be painted with
lively colors. Much can be said for and against such a
practice. I myself would not have the Venus of Milo
painted, but I would rather see a negro's head carved in
black marble than in white. On the whole my feeling is
that literary form ought to be in relation to the amount
of ideality which is spread over the representation. My
new drama is not indeed a tragedy in the old-world sig-
nification of the word, but what I have tried to depict in
it is human beings, and for that very reason I have not
allowed them to talk 'the language of the gods.' "

This severely realistic conception of what dramatic
form should be, a conception which sounded oddly at
first on the lips of a poet who had written impassioned
five-act plays entirely in elaborate rhymed measures, was
in strict harmony with the mental and moral tone of
the author in his new departure. Dr. Georg Brandes,
in his interesting volume " *Det Moderne Gjennembruds
Maend,*" has given us some valuable particulars regard-
ing Ibsen's political and philosophical experiences at
this crisis of his life. During the Franco-German war
it would seem that his sentiment with regard to life
and history underwent a complete revolution. He woke
up to see, or to think he saw, that we were living in
the last scene of the last act of a long drama; that all
which politics, morals, literature were giving us was but

the last and driest crumbs swept up from under the
table of eighteenth-century revolution ; that " Liberty,
equality, and fraternity " was played out as a motto, and
had come to mean the direct opposite of what it meant
to the "late lamented Guillotine." He saw, or thought
he saw, politicians wasting their energies on local and
superficial revolutions, not perceiving that all things
were making ready for a universal revolt of the spirit of
men. A few months later, in the following sentences,
he anticipated with a very surprising exactitude recent
utterances of Tolstoi. Ibsen wrote thus to Georg
Brandes :

"The State is the curse of the individual. How has
the national strength of Prussia been purchased ? By
the sinking of the individual in a political and geo-
graphical formula. . . . The State must go ! That
will be a revolution which will find me on its side.
Undermine the idea of the State, set up in its place
spontaneous action, and the idea that spiritual relation-
ship is the only thing that makes for unity, and you will
start the elements of a liberty which will be something
worth possessing."

It was in such a mood as this that Ibsen received
news of the Paris Commune with extreme disgust, re-
garding this caricature of his ideal as likely to delay
the realization of his genuine desire through at least a
generation. To await the new revolution, as religious
mystics await the solemn Second Advent, was now useless. The hope of the immediate future had sunk behind the Seine, and Ibsen turned from watching the
horizon to diagnose the symptoms of that mortal moral
disease, of which, as it appeared to him, Europe was

fast advancing toward social death. The hypocrisy of society and the brutality of personal egotism—these were the principal outward signs of that inward but universal malady which he saw the world sinking beneath. It was with no thought of reforming society, with no zeal of the missionary or the philanthropist, that he started on his new series of studies. He would spend the few years left to him before the political agony of Europe in noting down with an accuracy hitherto unparalleled the symptoms of her disorder. But with him always, since 1870, there has remained pre-eminent among his political convictions this belief, that the State is the natural enemy of the individual. Always an exile from his own country, he had settled in Dresden, rejoicing in the freedom of a small and uninfluential government. But in 1875, when Saxony became more and more identified with the vaunting glory and greatness of the Empire, he fled again. In a letter to me at that time he says : "I must go. In April I shall flit to Munich, and see if I can settle there for two or three years. I fancy that all spiritual life breathes with greater fulness and comfort there than here in North Germany, where the State and politics have drafted all the strength of the people into their service, and have arrested all genuine interests." Always this bogey of the State, paralyzing individual action, driving the poet through the cities of Europe to avoid the iron clangor of its wheels.

Such was, briefly, the mood in which Ibsen started the creation of his extraordinary series of social dramas. But in justice to another great poet we must not omit to acknowledge how much the field for the expression of these ideas was cleared for Ibsen by the dramas of Björnson. When the history of the Scandinavian literature of our age comes to be written, the rivalry between Björnson and Ibsen will form one of its most interesting pages. Björnson, although by several years the younger man, was famous first, and his name, in 1875, for instance, was certainly known to a dozen educated persons where but one had heard of Ibsen. He had, too, from an early age, taken a practical interest in the stage, and in the reform of dramatic literature. After writing saga-plays, like his rival, Björnson produced, in 1865, his short prose comedy of " *De Nygifte* " ("The Newly Married Couple"), where it is impossible to deny that in the character of Laura Aksel, the baby-wife, who loved her mother better than her husband, and has to be educated into individuality, there are features which curiously foreshadow Nora Helmer. In 1875 again, before Ibsen began his latest phase, Björnson published two prose plays, social and satirical dramas, the one of which, " *En Fallit* " (A Bankruptcy), deals with the ruin of a specious merchant, who is a pillar of the society of a little Norwegian seaport town ; the other, " *Redaktören* " (The Editor), deals with the part journalism, whether honest or the reverse, must take within the circle of limited municipalities. No reader of Ibsen but will be thinking at these words of " *The Pillars of Society*," of two years, and of " *The Enemy of Society*," of some years, later. In his " *Leonarda* " again, of 1879, Björnson treated the subject of the emancipation of the conscience from the conventional bonds of a traditional religion, a theme which long afterward became the centre of the action in Ibsen's " *Rosmersholm*." Again, but this time the order of production is reversed, in 1883 Björnson treated with great freedom, in his "*En Hanske*" (A Glove) some of those difficult sexual problems with which Ibsen had, in "*Ghosts*," so daringly grappled in 1881. Finally, he who can comprehend "*The Wild Duck*" of Ibsen may find in it a key to the still darker conundrums of Björnson's "*Over Ævne.*" In short, it would seem as if on almost all points the genius of these two poets had run in parallel lines, if with very different force and velocity. Nor will it do for an admirer of Ibsen to shrink from the fact that in almost all instances Björnson was first in the field. It is none the less a fact that Björnson's talent, as a playwright, is far less stimulating and important than that of Ibsen, between which and the customary products of Scandinavian drama it is chiefly interesting as forming a link.

From the earliest manifestations of his peculiar genius the best critics have perceived in Ibsen a certain smouldering fire which has sufficed to make remarkable the crudest and least satisfactory of his productions. Björnson's is a charming talent, but Björnson has nothing of this secret and devouring flame of passion. However, when a comparison is made between those plays of his which have just been mentioned and those later dramas of Ibsen's which they might seem to have suggested, there is found to be little real similarity between them, Björnson is a frank republican, opposed to kings and priests on principle, and ready to take a personal part in setting up a revolutionized form of government. To Ibsen all existing forms of government lie under suspicion, and the President of a Norse Republic delights not

2

him. Björnson perceives certain absurdities in our existing code of sexual morality, and cheerfully proposes to
modify manners. To Ibsen the whole conventional relation of the sexes is sinister and fraught with dangerous
possibilities. Björnson is dissatisfied with certain conditions of Scandinavian Lutheranism; to Ibsen all the
ethics of religion seem about to be arraigned before the
bar of humanity. The younger poet wishes to sweep
and garnish the house; the elder is questioning within
himself whether it would not be best, as the Persian
poet says,

> " To grasp this sorry scheme of things entire,
>   . . .   to shatter it to bits—and then
> Remould it nearer to the Heart's Desire."

To an American audience it would seem as though
Ibsen should speak with greater certainty of a sympa-
thetic hearing than to any other. In no European
poet except himself do we find the problems of advanced
democracy faced with so much courage or with so little rhetoric. The fanfarons of Victor Hugo seem old-
fashioned and ineffectual, the audacities of Carducci and
of Swinburne are like the sport of aristocratic children
beside the gravity, the terse and stern attitude of arrest,
which we meet with in Ibsen's prose dramas. The provincial atmosphere, the air of the little market-town in
some country part of Norway, merely deepens the sense
of strenuousness, as the earnestness of a countryman
may put to shame a metropolitan frivolity. His seven
plays are seven arrows in the heart of the mundane god-
dess of modern society. Whether it is commercial hypocrisy, as in "*The Pillars of Society;*" or the sacrifice

of feminine individuality, as in "*A Doll's House;*" or the hatred of truth, as in "*The Enemy of Society;*" whether it is the sins of the fathers, as in "*Ghosts;*" or the phantom of conventional religion, as in "*Rosmersholm;*" or the brittle shell of humanitarian optimism, as in "*The Wild Duck;*" or the tenuity of the marriage tie, as in "*The Lady from the Sea,*" in each case a sword is driven between the bone and the marrow of modern life. Ibsen is the enemy of all convention; he takes nothing for granted. No axiom is so universally received as to be safe from his profane analysis.

Close as we are to the production of Ibsen's plays, we can hardly perhaps judge very rightly yet of the fabric which is actually being wound off the loom under our very eyes. But some things we can plainly see, and among them the absolute novelty of this new species of dramatic literature. One very interesting feature of Ibsen's work is the relation it holds to the modern novel. For the last half-century and more, the novel, in almost all countries, has been leaving the literary drama far behind it in point of interest. In France alone the drama has retained something of its old literary pre-eminence. A play of the younger Dumas holds its own by the side of a novel of the same author. A new comedy by Pailleron is read, even though a new novel by Manupassant makes its appearance. Nevertheless, in France itself, the literature of drama is less and less able to cope with the literature of fiction. In England and America, of course, the former is not in the background so much as it is positively non-existent. In Scandinavia, to a less extent, the same has been the case. Björnson's plays

have not successfully competed with Björnson's novels ;
but Ibsen's dramas do compete successfully with their
most dangerous rivals in fiction, the novels of Alexander
Kjelland.   The reason of this general decline of the read
play is, as all critics admit, the increased conventionality
of the stage, and if Ibsen has succeeded where others
have failed, it is because he is essentially less conventional than others.

Ibsen has created a new form of drama, and until he is
himself superseded by some still more vivid painter of
actual life, we must look upon him as the first of dramatic realists.   The impression of vitality, of actuality,
which his plays give us arises partly from the truth of
his dialogue, which is astonishing, and partly from the
alteration of plan which he has introduced.   All plays
before his are built on the system of climbing up the
hill to a crisis and then rushing downward.   The " well-
made " comedy of Scribe or of Sardou has reduced this
Jack-and-Jill ideal of dramatic construction to a me-
chanical trick.   The figures are drawn up to the apex of
their intrigue with a string, and dropped down the in-
clined plane at a given signal.   But with Ibsen the down
ward path has been taken before the play opens, and the
velocity is cumulative from the first scene to the last.
The false position of Consul Bernick is finally taken before the curtain rises ; nothing can involve Nora in
deeper embarrassment than what has already happened ;
the last hour of the destiny of the house of Rosmer has
struck ; the popularity of Stockmann is compromised
beyond all hope, the poison is already in the bones of
Oswald Alving.   The poet constructs no artificial edifice.
He conducts his readers breathlessly down toward the

inevitable catastrophe, and what is of pre-eminent interest to him is not the primary circumstances but their consequent results. In this analysis of fatal consequences he has been thought more to resemble Sophocles than any of the moderns. This method, at all events, is wholly unlike that of the two ever-recurring models of modern poetic or artificial drama, Shakespeare and Molière. It would really seem as though Ibsen had added a new branch to dramatic literature by inventing the drama of catastrophe.

The quality which has lifted these dramas out of the range of the literature that interests scholars and the curious, that element in them which has so strangely and intimately appealed, in all the countries of Europe, to discontented, solitary, agitated, and unfortunate persons, is the frank dissatisfaction which they express. All who are not optimistic, all whose ideal is not to be "proper" and listen to what the squire says on weekdays and the clergyman on Sundays ; all who, without wish for rebellion, feel their life bathed in a revolutionary atmosphere, and all whose ideals are broken and their illusions evaporated, come to the plays of Ibsen as to a cave of Adullam. It is not that he has a panacea for their woes ; it is not that he has a ready-made answer to the conundrums that trouble them ; but that he seems like themselves. They are poor, and he is not dazzled by or enamoured of wealth. They are angry with fortune, and he is no courter of her favors. They are groaning under conventional burdens, and he claims from them nothing but to be natural. They are driven in the mass of modern democracy, ticketed and numbered in the foundling hospital of life, and he is the apologist of the individual conscience. It is an entire mistake to look upon Ibsen as a conscious teacher. The inevitable, priggishness of the apostle is missing in him. His method is Socratic. " Let us talk it over," he seems to say ; " let us analyze the position ; let us take a typical case and see how it works out." We learn, but he persuades us that it is not he, but Nature, who is our schoolmaster.

Ibsen appears to me to be so great and so new that the first and most essential step to be taken in reading him seems to be to try to reach the secret of his novelty and his greatness. I have, therefore, not alluded here to features in his work which still do not quite tally with our preconceived standards of perfection. His plays sometimes seem crude in construction ; " *The Wild Duck,*" in its revolt against the " well-made " drama, is positively ill-made. He has never quite abandoned his tendency to lose his dramatic person in a bodiless trait of character. His realism, like that of all pronounced realists, has a trick of being excessively unreal, as, for instance, in the development of Oswald's disease in " *Ghosts,*" and in the whole conception of the Strange Man in " *The Lady from the Sea.*" But if the realists never lapsed into romanticism what would become of us all, and Ibsen shall never be reproached for his inability to forget that he is a poet. His peculiar merits and powers must now be left, in the admirable versions which are here presented to the public, to make their own impression. Those who desire to account for Ibsen's recent eminence and the curiosity with which his plays have been of late regarded, may find the reason in an old couplet of Dryden's which says :

"They who have best succeeded on the stage
Have still conformed their genius to their age."

Whatever is unsettled, sinister, and critical in this close of the nineteenth century has at least found an exponent in the author of " Ghosts " and of " A Doll's House."

EDMUND GOSSE.

A DOLL'S HOUSE

A PLAY IN THREE ACTS

BY

HENRIK IBSEN

TRANSLATED BY WILLIAM ARCHER

TRANSLATOR'S NOTE.

The following pages contain the complete text of "Et Dukkehjem." A few passages omitted, for the sake of compression, from the version produced at the Novelty Theatre, London, have been scrupulously restored. Otherwise the text of that version is almost literally adhered to. I have to express my obligations, in the first place, to the previous rendering of the play by Miss Frances Lord, which afforded many suggestions; in the second place, to Miss Janet Achurch and Mr. Charles Charrington, who gave me most valuable assistance in revising my original draft.

                                                    W. A.

CHARACTERS.

TORVALD HELMER.
NORA HELMER.
DR. RANK.
NILS KROGSTAD.
MRS. LINDEN.
ANNA,
ELLEN, } *Servants.*
IVAR,
EMMY, } *The Helmers' Children.*
BOB,

SCENE: *Sitting-room in* HELMER'S *House (a flat) in Christiania.*

TIME: *The Present Day; Christmastide.*

The action takes place on three consecutive days.

opening scene
is winter

A DOLL'S HOUSE.

ACT I.

[*A room comfortably and tastefully, but not expensively, furnished. In the background, to the right, a door leads to the hall; to the left, another door leads to* HELMER's *study. Between the two doors a pianoforte. In the middle of the left wall, a door, and nearer the front a window. Near the window a round table with armchairs and a small sofa. In the right wall, somewhat to the back, a door; and against the same wall, farther forward, a porcelain stove; in front of it a couple of armchairs and a rocking-chair. Between the stove and the side door a small table. Engravings on the walls. A whatnot with china and bric-à-brac. A small book-case of showily bound books. Carpet. A fire in the stove. A winter day.*]

[*A bell rings in the hall outside. Presently the outer door is heard to open. Then* NORA *enters, humming contentedly. She is in out-door dress, and carries several parcels, which she lays on the right-hand table. She leaves the door into the hall open behind her, and a* PORTER *is seen outside, carrying a Christmas-tree and a basket, which he gives to the maid-servant who has opened the door.*]

opening scene,
describes setting
and Nora's entrance

NORA. Hide the Christmas-tree carefully, Ellen ; the children mustn't see it before this evening, when it's lighted up. (*To the* PORTER, *taking out her purse.*) How much ?

PORTER. Fifty öre.*

NORA. There's a crown. No, keep the change. (*The* PORTER *thanks her and goes.* NORA *shuts the door. She continues smiling in quiet glee as she takes off her walking things. Then she takes from her pocket a bag of macaroons, and eats one or two. As she does so, she goes on tip-toe to her husband's door and listens.*)

NORA. Yes ; he is at home. (*She begins humming again, going to the table on the right.*)

HELMER (*in his room*). Is that my lark twittering there ?

NORA (*busy opening some of her parcels*). Yes, it is.

HELMER. Is it the squirrel skipping about ?

NORA. Yes !

HELMER. When did the squirrel get home ?

NORA. Just this minute. (*Hides the bag of macaroons in her pocket and wipes her mouth.*) Come here, Torvald, and see what I've bought.

HELMER. Don't disturb me. (*A little later he opens the door and looks in, pen in hand.*) "Bought," did you say ? What ! all that ? Has my little spendthrift been making the money fly again ?

NORA. Why, Torvald, surely we can afford to launch out a little now ! It's the first Christmas we haven't had to pinch.

HELMER. Come, come ; we can't afford to squander money.

* About sixpence. There are 100 öre in a krone or crown, which is worth thirteenpence halfpenny.

NORA. Oh, yes, Torvald, do let us squander a little—just the least little bit, won't you? You know you'll soon be earning heaps of money.

HELMER. Yes, from New Year's Day. But there's a whole quarter before my first salary is due.

NORA. Never mind; we can borrow in the meantime.

HELMER. Nora! (*He goes up to her and takes her playfully by the ear.*) Thoughtless as ever! Supposing I borrowed a thousand crowns to-day, and you spent it during Christmas week, and that on New Year's Eve a tile blew off the roof and knocked my brains out——

NORA (*laying her hand on his mouth*). Hush! How can you talk so horridly?

HELMER. But, supposing it were to happen—what then?

NORA. If anything so dreadful happened, I shouldn't care whether I was in debt or not.

HELMER. But what about the creditors?

NORA. They! Who cares for them? They're only strangers.

HELMER. Nora, Nora! What a woman you are! But seriously, Nora, you know my ideas on these points. No debts! No credit! Home-life ceases to be free and beautiful as soon as it is founded on borrowing and debt. We two have held out bravely till now, and we won't give in at the last.

NORA (*going to the fireplace*). Very well—as you like, Torvald.

HELMER (*following her*). Come, come; my little lark mustn't let her wings droop like that. What? Is the squirrel pouting there? (*Takes out his purse.*) Nora, what do you think I've got here?

NORA (*turning round quickly*). Money !

HELMER. There ! (*Gives her some notes.*) Of course I know all sorts of things are wanted at Christmas.

NORA (*counting*). Ten, twenty, thirty, forty. Oh ! thank you, thank you, Torvald. This will go a long way.

HELMER. I should hope so.

NORA. Yes, indeed, a long way ! But come here, and see all I've been buying. And so cheap ! Look, here is a new suit for Ivar, and a little sword. Here are a horse and a trumpet for Bob. And here are a doll and a cradle for Emmy. They're only common ; but she'll soon pull them all to pieces. And dresses and neckties for the servants ; only I should have got something better for dear old Anna.

HELMER. And what's in that other parcel ?

NORA (*crying out*). No, Torvald, you're not to see that until this evening.

HELMER. Oh ! ah ! But now tell me, you little rogue, what have you got for yourself ?

NORA. For myself ? Oh, I don't want anything.

HELMER. Nonsense. Just tell me something sensible you would like to have.

NORA. No. Really I want nothing. . . . Well, listen, Torvald——

HELMER. Well ?

NORA (*playing with his coat buttons, without looking him in the face*). If you really want to give me something, you might, you know, you might——

HELMER. Well, well ? Out with it !

NORA (*quickly*). You might give me money, Torvald. Only just what you think you can spare ; then I can buy myself something with it later.

HELMER. But, Nora——

NORA. Oh, please do, dear Torvald, please do! Then I would hang the money in lovely gilt paper on the Christmas-tree. Wouldn't that be fun?

HELMER. What do they call the birds that are always making the money fly?

NORA. Yes, I know—spendthrifts,* of course. But please do as I say, Torvald. Then I shall have time to think what I want most. Isn't that very sensible, now?

HELMER (*smiling*). Certainly; that is to say, if you really kept the money I gave you, and really bought yourself something with it. But it all goes in house-keeping, and for all sorts of useless things, and then I have to find more.

NORA. But, Torvald——

HELMER. Can you deny it, Nora dear? (*He puts his arm round her.*) It's a sweet little lark; but it gets through a lot of money. No one would believe how much it costs a man to keep such a little bird as you.

condescending

NORA. For shame! how can you say so? Why, I save as much as ever I can.

HELMER (*laughing*). Very true—as much as you can—but you can't.

NORA (*hums and smiles in quiet satisfaction*). H'm!— you should just know, Torvald, what expenses we larks and squirrels have.

—the "doll"

HELMER. You're a strange little being! Just like your father—always eager to get hold of money; but the moment you have it, it seems to slip through your fingers; you never know what becomes of it. Well, one must

* *Spillefugl*, literally, " playbird," means a gambler

3

take you as you are. It's in the blood. Yes, Nora, that sort of thing is inherited.

NORA. I wish I had inherited many of my father's qualities.

HELMER. And I don't wish you anything but just what you are—my own, sweet little song-bird. But, I say— it strikes me—you look so, so—what shall I call it?—so suspicious to-day——

NORA. Do I?

HELMER. You do, indeed. Look me full in the face.

NORA (*looking at him*). Well?

HELMER (*threatening with his finger*). Hasn't the little sweet-tooth been breaking the rules to-day?

NORA. No; how can you think of such a thing !

HELMER. Didn't she just look in at the confectioner's ?

NORA. No, Torvald, really——

HELMER. Not to sip a little jelly?

NORA. No; certainly not.

HELMER. Hasn't she even nibbled a macaroon or two ?

NORA. No, Torvald, indeed, indeed !

HELMER. Well, well, well; of course I'm only joking.

NORA (*goes to the table on the right*). I shouldn't think of doing what you disapprove of.

HELMER. No, I'm sure of that; and, besides, you've given me your word. (*Going toward her.*) Well, keep your little Christmas secrets to yourself, Nora darling. The Christmas-tree will bring them all to light, I daresay.

NORA. Have you remembered to ask Doctor Rank ?

HELMER. No. But it's not necessary ; he'll come as a matter of course. Besides, I shall invite him when he looks in to-day. I've ordered some capital wine. Nora, you can't think how I look forward to this evening !

NORA. And I too. How the children will enjoy themselves, Torvald!

HELMER. Ah! it's glorious to feel that one has an assured position and ample means. Isn't it delightful to think of?

NORA. Oh, it's wonderful!

HELMER. Do you remember last Christmas? For three whole weeks beforehand you shut yourself up till long past midnight to make flowers for the Christmas-tree, and all sorts of other marvels that were to have astonished us. I was never so bored in my life.

NORA. I did not bore myself at all.

HELMER (*smiling*). And it came to so little after all, Nora.

NORA. Oh! are you going to tease me about that again? How could I help the cat getting in and spoil it all?

HELMER. To be sure you couldn't, my poor little Nora. You did your best to amuse us all, and that's the main thing. But, all the same, it's a good thing the hard times are over.

NORA. Oh, isn't it wonderful!

HELMER. Now, I needn't sit here boring myself all alone; and you needn't tire your dear eyes and your delicate little fingers——

NORA (*clapping her hands*). No, I needn't, need I, Torvald? Oh! it's wonderful to think of! (*Takes his arm.*) And now I'll tell you how I think we ought to manage, Torvald. As soon as Christmas is over—— (*The hall-door bell rings.*) Oh, there's a ring! (*Arranging the room.*) That's somebody come to call. How vexing!

HELMER. I am "not at home" to callers; remember that.

ELLEN (*in the doorway*). A lady to see you, ma'am.

NORA. Show her in.

ELLEN (*to* HELMER). And the Doctor is just come, sir.

HELMER. Has he gone into my study?

ELLEN. Yes, sir.

HELMER *goes into his study.* ELLEN *ushers in* MRS. LINDEN *in travelling costume, and shuts the door behind her.*

MRS. LINDEN (*timidly and hesitatingly*). How do you do, Nora?

NORA (*doubtfully*). How do you do?

MRS. LINDEN. I daresay you don't recognize me?

NORA. No, I don't think—oh, yes!—I believe—— (*Effusively.*) What! Christina! Is it really you?

MRS. LINDEN. Yes; really I!

NORA. Christina! and to think I didn't know you! But how could I—— (*More softly.*) How changed you are, Christina!

MRS. LINDEN. Yes, no doubt. In nine or ten years——

NORA. Is it really so long since we met? Yes, so it is. Oh! the last eight years have been a happy time, I can tell you. And now you have come to town? All that long journey in mid-winter! How brave of you.

MRS. LINDEN. I arrived by this morning's steamer.

NORA. To keep Christmas, of course. Oh, how delightful! What fun we shall have! Take your things off. Aren't you frozen? (*Helping her.*) There, now we'll sit down here cosily by the fire. No, you take the arm-chair; I'll sit in this rocking-chair. (*Seizes her hand.*) Yes, now I can see the dear old face again. It was only at the first glance—— But you're a little paler, Christina, and perhaps a little thinner.

MRS. LINDEN. And much, much older, Nora.

NORA. Yes, perhaps a little older—not much—ever so little. (*She suddenly stops ; seriously.*) Oh ! what a thoughtless wretch I am ! Here I sit chattering on, and ——Dear, dear Christina, can you forgive me ?

MRS. LINDEN. What do you mean, Nora ?

NORA (*softly*). Poor Christina ! I forgot, you are a widow ?

MRS. LINDEN. Yes ; my husband died three years ago.

NORA. I know, I know, I saw it in the papers. Oh ! believe me, Christina, I did mean to write to you ; but I kept putting it off, and something always came in the way.

MRS. LINDEN. I can quite understand that, Nora dear.

NORA. No, Christina ; it was horrid of me. Oh, you poor darling ! how much you must have gone through ! —and he left you nothing ?

MRS. LINDEN. Nothing.

NORA. And no children?

MRS. LINDEN. None.

NORA. Nothing, nothing at all ?

MRS. LINDEN. Not even a sorrow or a longing to dwell upon.

NORA (*looking at her incredulously*). My dear Christina, how is that possible ?

MRS. LINDEN (*smiling sadly and stroking her hair*). Oh, it happens sometimes, Nora.

NORA. So utterly alone. How dreadful that must be ! I have three of the loveliest children. I can't show them to you just now ; they're out with their nurse. But now you must tell me everything.

MRS. LINDEN. No, no, I want you to tell me——

NORA. No, you must begin ; I won't be egotistical to-day. To-day, I will think of you only. Oh! I must tell you one thing ; but perhaps you've heard of our great stroke of fortune ?

MRS. LINDEN. No.   What is it?

NORA. Only think! my husband has been made Manager of the Joint Stock Bank.

MRS. LINDEN. Your husband!   Oh, how fortunate!

NORA. Yes, isn't it?   A lawyer's position is so uncertain, you see, especially when he won't touch any business that's the least bit . . .   shady, as of course Torvald won't; and in that I quite agree with him. Oh! you can imagine how glad we are. He is to enter on his new position at the New Year, and then he will have a large salary, and percentages.   In future we shall be able to live quite differently—just as we please, in fact. Oh, Christina, I feel so light and happy! It's splendid to have lots of money, and no need to worry about things, isn't it ?

MRS. LINDEN. Yes ; it must be delightful to have what you need.

NORA. No, not only what you need, but heaps of money—heaps!

MRS. LINDEN (*smiling*). Nora, Nora, haven't you learnt reason yet ?   In our schooldays you were a shocking little spendthrift!

NORA (*quietly smiling*). Yes ; Torvald says I am still. (*Threatens with her finger.*) But "Nora, Nora," is not so silly as you all think. Oh! I haven't had the chance to be much of a spendthrift. We have both had to work.

MRS. LINDEN. You too?

NORA. Yes, light fancy work; crochet, and embroidery, and things of that sort, (*significantly*) and other work too. You know, of course, that Torvald left the Government service when we were married. He had little chance of promotion, and of course he required to make more money. But in the first year of our marriage he overworked himself terribly. He had to undertake all sorts of odd jobs, you know, and to work early and late. He couldn't stand it, and fell dangerously ill. Then the doctors declared he must go to the South.

MRS. LINDEN. Yes; you spent a whole year in Italy, didn't you?

NORA. We did. It wasn't easy to manage, I can tell you. It was just after Ivar's birth. But of course we had to go. Oh, it was a delicious journey! And it saved Torvald's life. But it cost a frightful lot of money, Christina.

MRS. LINDEN. So I should think.

NORA. Twelve hundred dollars! Four thousand eight hundred crowns! Isn't that a lot of money?

MRS. LINDEN. How lucky you had the money to spend!

NORA. I must tell you we got it from father.

MRS. LINDEN. Ah, I see. He died just about that time, didn't he?

NORA. Yes, Christina, just then. And only think! I couldn't go and nurse him! I was expecting little Ivar's birth daily. And then I had my Torvald to attend to. Dear, kind old father! I never saw him again, Christina. Oh! that's the hardest thing I've had to bear since my marriage.

MRS. LINDEN. I know how fond you were of him. And then you went to Italy?

NORA. Yes; we had the money, and the doctors insisted. We started a month later.

MRS. LINDEN. And your husband returned completely cured?

NORA. Sound as a bell.

MRS. LINDEN. But—the doctor?

NORA. What about him?

MRS. LINDEN. I thought as I came in your servant announced the Doctor——

NORA. Oh, yes; Doctor Rank. But he doesn't come as a doctor. He's our best friend, and never lets a day pass without looking in. No, Torvald hasn't had an hour's illness since that time. And the children are so healthy and well, and so am I. (*Jumps up and claps her hands.*) Oh, Christina, Christina, it's so lovely to live and to be happy!—Oh! but it's really too horrid of me! —Here am I talking about nothing but my own concerns. (*Sits down upon a footstool close to her and lays her arms on* CHRISTINA's *lap.*) Oh! don't be angry with me! —Now just tell me, is it really true that you didn't love your husband? What made you take him?

MRS. LINDEN. My mother was then alive, bedridden and helpless; and I had my two younger brothers to think of. I thought it my duty to accept him.

NORA. Perhaps it was. I suppose he was rich then?

MRS. LINDEN. Very well off, I believe. But his business was uncertain. It fell to pieces at his death, and there was nothing left.

NORA. And then——?

MRS. LINDEN. Then I had to fight my way by keeping a shop, a little school, anything I could turn my hand to. The last three years have been one long struggle for me. But now it's over, Nora. My poor mother no longer needs me ; she is at rest. And the boys are in business, and can look after themselves.

NORA. How free your life must feel !

MRS. LINDEN. No, Nora ; only inexpressibly empty. No one to live for. (*Stands up restlessly.*) That is why I couldn't bear to stay any longer in that out-of-the-way corner. Here it must be easier to find something really worth doing—something to occupy one's thoughts. If I could only get some settled employment—some office-work.

NORA. But, Christina, that's so tiring, and you look worn out already. You should rather go to some watering-place and rest.

MRS. LINDEN (*going to the window*). I have no father to give me the money, Nora.

NORA (*rising*). Oh ! don't be vexed with me.

MRS. LINDEN (*going toward her*). My dear Nora, don't you be vexed with me. The worst of a position like mine is that it makes one bitter. You have no one to work for, yet you have to be always on the strain. You must live ; and so you become selfish. When I heard of the happy change in your circumstances—can you believe it ?—I rejoiced more on my own account than on yours.

NORA. How do you mean? Ah! I see. You mean Torvald could perhaps do something for you.

MRS. LINDEN. Yes ; I thought so.

NORA. And so he shall, Christina. Just you leave it all to me. I shall lead up to it beautifully, and think of something pleasant to put him in a good humor! Oh! I should so love to do something for you.

MRS. LINDEN. How good of you, Nora! And doubly good in you, who know so little of the troubles of life.

NORA. I? I know so little of——?

MRS. LINDEN (*smiling*). Ah, well! a little fancy-work, and so forth. You're a mere child, Nora.

NORA (*tosses her head and paces the room*). Oh, come, you mustn't be so patronizing!

MRS. LINDEN. No?

NORA. You're like the rest. You all think I'm fit for nothing really serious——

MRS. LINDEN. Well——

NORA. You think I've had no troubles in this weary world.

MRS. LINDEN. My dear Nora, you've just told me all your troubles.

NORA. Pooh—these trifles. (*Softly.*) I haven't told you the great thing.

MRS. LINDEN. The great thing? What do you mean?

NORA. I know you look down upon me, Christina ; but you've no right to. You're proud of having worked so hard and so long for your mother?

MRS. LINDEN. I'm sure I don't look down upon anyone ; but it's true I'm both proud and glad when I remember that I was able to make my mother's last days free from care.

NORA. And you're proud to think of what you have done for your brothers?

MRS. LINDEN. Have I not the right to be?

NORA. Yes, surely. But now let me tell you Christina—I, too, have something to be proud and glad of.

MRS. LINDEN. I don't doubt it. But what do you mean?

NORA. Hush! Not so loud. Only think, if Torvald were to hear! He mustn't—not for worlds! No one must know about it, Christina—no one but you.

MRS. LINDEN. What can it be?

NORA. Come over here. (*Draws her beside her on the sofa.*) Yes—I, too, have something to be proud and glad of. *I* saved Torvald's life.

MRS. LINDEN. Saved his life? How?

NORA. I told you about our going to Italy. Torvald would have died but for that.

MRS. LINDEN. Yes—and your father gave you the money.

NORA (*smiling*). Yes, so Torvald and everyone believes; but——

MRS. LINDEN. But—— ?

NORA. Father didn't give us one penny. *I* found the money.

MRS. LINDEN. You? All that money?

NORA. Twelve hundred dollars. Four thousand eight hundred crowns. What do you say to that?

MRS. LINDEN. My dear Nora, how did you manage it? Did you win it in the lottery?

NORA (*contemptuously*). In the lottery? Pooh! Any fool could have done that!

MRS. LINDEN. Then wherever did you get it from?

NORA (*hums and smiles mysteriously*). H'm; tra-la-la-la!

MRS. LINDEN. Of course you couldn't borrow it.

NORA. No? Why not?

MRS. LINDEN. Why, a wife can't borrow without her husband's consent.

NORA (*tossing her head*). Oh! when the wife knows a little of business, and how to set about things, then——

MRS. LINDEN. But, Nora, I don't understand——

NORA. Well you needn't. I never said I borrowed the money. Perhaps I got it another way. (*Throws herself back on the sofa.*) I may have got it from some admirer. When one is so—attractive as I am——

MRS. LINDEN. You're too silly, Nora.

NORA. Now I'm sure you're dying of curiosity, Christina——

MRS. LINDEN. Listen to me, Nora dear. Haven't you been a little rash?

NORA (*sitting upright again*). Is it rash to save one's husband's life?

MRS. LINDEN. I think it was rash of you, without his knowledge——

NORA. But it would have been fatal for him to know! Can't you understand that? He was never to suspect how ill he was. The doctors came to me privately and told me that his life was in danger—that nothing could save him but a trip to the South. Do you think I didn't try diplomacy first? I told him how I longed to have a trip abroad, like other young wives; I wept and prayed; I said he ought to think of my condition, and not thwart me; and then I hinted that he could borrow the money. But then, Christina, he got almost angry. He said I was frivolous, and that it was his duty as a husband not to yield to my whims and fancies—so he called them. Very well, thought I, but saved you must be; and then I found the way to do it.

MRS. LINDEN. And did your husband never learn from your father that the money was not from him?

NORA. No; never. Father died at that very time. I

meant to have told him all about it, and begged him to say nothing. But he was so ill—unhappily, it was not necessary.

MRS. LINDEN. And you have never confessed to your husband?

NORA. Good Heavens! What can you be thinking of? Tell him, when he has such a loathing of debt? And besides—how painful and humiliating it would be for Torvald, with his manly self-reliance, to know that he owed anything to me! It would utterly upset the relation between us; our beautiful, happy home would never again be what it is.

MRS. LINDEN. Will you never tell him?

NORA (*thoughtfully, half-smiling*). Yes, some time perhaps—after many years, when I'm—not so pretty. You mustn't laugh at me. Of course I mean when Torvald is not so much in love with me as he is now; when it doesn't amuse him any longer to see me skipping about, and dressing up and acting. Then it might be well to have something in reserve. (*Breaking off.*) Nonsense! nonsense! That time will never come. Now, what do you say to my grand secret, Christina? Am I fit for nothing now? You may believe it has cost me a lot of anxiety. It has been no joke to meet my engagements punctually. You must know, Christina, that in business there are things called instalments and quarterly interest, that are terribly hard to meet. So I had to pinch a little here and there, wherever I could. I could not save anything out of the housekeeping, for of course Torvald had to live well. And I couldn't let the children go about badly dressed; all I got for them, I spent on them, the darlings.

MRS. LINDEN. Poor Nora! So it had to come out of your own pocket-money.

NORA. Yes, of course. After all, the whole thing was my doing. When Torvald gave me money for clothes and so on, I never used more than half of it; I always bought the simplest things. It's a mercy everything suits me so well; Torvald never noticed anything. But it was often very hard, Christina dear. For it's nice to be beautifully dressed. Now, isn't it?

MRS. LINDEN. Indeed it is.

NORA. Well, and besides that, I made money in other ways. Last winter I was so lucky—I got a heap of copying to do. I shut myself up every evening and wrote far on into the night. Oh, sometimes I was so tired, so tired. And yet it was splendid to work in that way and earn money. I almost felt as if I was a man.

MRS. LINDEN. Then how much have you been able to pay off?

NORA. Well, I can't precisely say. It's difficult to keep that sort of business clear. I only know that I paid off everything I could scrape together. Sometimes I really didn't know where to turn. (*Smiles.*) Then I used to imagine that a rich old gentleman was in love with me——

MRS. LINDEN. What! What gentleman?

NORA. Oh! nobody—that he was now dead, and that when his will was opened, there stood in large letters: Pay over at once everything of which I die possessed to that charming person, Mrs. Nora Helmer.

MRS. LINDEN. But, dear Nora, what gentleman do you mean?

NORA. Dear, dear, can't you understand? There

wasn't any old gentleman : it was only what I used to dream, and dream when I was at my wit's end for money. But it's all over now—the tiresome old creature may stay where he is for me ; I care nothing for him or his will ; for now my troubles are over. (*Springing up.*) Oh, Christina, how glorious it is to think of? Free from cares! Free, quite free. To be able to play and romp about with the children ; to have things tasteful and pretty in the house, exactly as Torvald likes it! And then the spring is coming, with the great blue sky. Perhaps then we shall have a short holiday. Perhaps I shall see the sea again. Oh, what a wonderful thing it is to live and to be happy! (*The hall door-bell rings.*)

MRS. LINDEN (*rising*). There is a ring. Perhaps I had better go.

NORA. No ; do stay. It's sure to be some one for Torvald.

ELLEN (*in the doorway*). If you please, ma'am, there's a gentleman to speak to Mr. Helmer.

NORA. Who is the gentleman?

KROGSTAD (*in the doorway to the hall*). It is I Mrs. Helmer. (ELLEN *goes.* MRS. LINDEN *starts and turns away to the window.*)

NORA (*goes a step toward him, anxiously, half aloud*). You? What is it? What do you want with my husband?

KROGSTAD. Bank business—in a way. I hold a small post in the Joint Stock Bank, and your husband is to be our new chief, I hear.

NORA. Then it is——?

KROGSTAD. Only tiresome business, Mrs. Helmer ; nothing more.

NORA. Then will you please go to his study. (KROG-STAD *goes.* *She bows indifferently while she closes the door into the hall.* *Then she goes to the fireplace and looks to the fire.*)

MRS. LINDEN. Nora—who was that man?

NORA. A Mr. Krogstad. Do you know him?

MRS. LINDEN. I used to know him—many years ago. He was in a lawyer's office in our town.

NORA. Yes, so he was.

MRS. LINDEN. How he has changed !

NORA. I believe his marriage was unhappy.

MRS. LINDEN. And he is now a widower?

NORA. With a lot of children. There ! now it'll burn up. (*She closes the stove, and pushes the rocking-chair a little aside.*)

MRS. LINDEN. His business is not of the most credit-able, they say.

NORA. Isn't it ? I daresay not. I don't know—— But don't let us think of business—it's so tiresome.

DR. RANK *comes out of* HELMER's *room.*

RANK (*still in the doorway*). No, no; I won't keep you. I'll just go and have a chat with your wife. (*Shuts the door and sees* MRS. LINDEN.) Oh, I beg your pardon. I am *de trop* here too.

NORA. No, not in the least. (*Introduces them.*) Doc-tor Rank—Mrs. Linden.

RANK. Oh, indeed; I've often heard Mrs. Linden's name. I think I passed you on the stairs as we came up.

MRS. LINDEN. Yes ; I go so very slowly. Stairs try me so much.

RANK. You're not very strong ?

MRS. LINDEN. Only overworked.

RANK. Ah! Then you have come to town to find rest in a round of dissipation.

MRS. LINDEN. I have come to look for employment.

RANK. Is that an approved remedy for over-work?

MRS. LINDEN. One must live, Doctor Rank.

RANK. Yes, that seems to be the general opinion.

NORA. Come, Doctor Rank, you yourself want to live.

RANK. To be sure I do. However wretched I may be, I want to drag on as long as possible. And my patients have all the same mania. It's just the same with people whose complaint is moral. At this very moment Helmer is talking to such a wreck as I mean.

MRS. LINDEN (*softly*). Ah!

NORA. Whom do you mean?

RANK. Oh, a fellow named Krogstad, a man you know nothing about—corrupt to the very core of his character. But even he began by announcing solemnly that he must live.

NORA. Indeed? Then what did he want with Torvald?

RANK. I really don't know; I only gathered that it was some Bank business.

NORA. I didn't know that Krog—that this Mr. Krogstad had anything to do with the Bank?

RANK. He has some sort of place there. (*To* MRS. LINDEN.) I don't know whether, in your part of the country, you have people who go wriggling and snuffing around in search of moral rottenness—whose policy it is to fill good places with men of tainted character whom they can keep under their eye and in their power? The honest men they leave out in the cold.

4

MRS. LINDEN. Well, I suppose the—delicate characters require most care.

RANK (*shrugs his shoulders*). There we have it ! It's that notion that makes society a hospital. (NORA, *deep in her own thoughts, breaks into half-stifled laughter and claps her hands.*) What are you laughing at ? Have you any idea what society is?

NORA. What do I care for your tiresome society. I was laughing at something else—something awfully amusing. Tell me, Doctor Rank, are all the employees at the Bank dependent on Torvald now?

RANK. Is that what strikes you as awfully amusing?

NORA (*smiles and hums*). Never mind, never mind ! (*Walks about the room.*) Yes, it *is* amusing to think that we—that Torvald has such power over so many people. (*Takes the box from her pocket.*) Doctor Rank, will you have a macaroon ?

RANK. Oh, dear, dear—macaroons ! I thought they were contraband here.

NORA. Yes ; but Christina brought me these.

MRS. LINDEN. What ! I?

NORA. Oh, well ! Don't be frightened. You couldn't possibly know that Torvald had forbidden them. The fact is, he is afraid of me spoiling my teeth. But, oh bother, just for once. That's for you, Doctor Rank ! (*Puts a macaroon into his mouth.*) And you, too, Christina. And I will have one at the same time—only a tiny one, or at most two. (*Walks about again.*) Oh, dear, I am happy ! There is only one thing in the world that I really want.

RANK. Well ; what's that?

NORA. There's something I should so like to say—in Torvald's hearing.

RANK. Then why don't you say it?

NORA. Because I daren't, it's so ugly.

MRS. LINDEN. Ugly?

RANK. In that case you'd better not. But to us you might. What is it you would so like to say in Helmer's hearing?

NORA. I should so love to say—"Damn!"*

RANK. Are you out of your mind?

MRS. LINDEN. Good gracious, Nora!

RANK. Say it. There he is!

NORA (*hides the macaroons*). Hush-sh-sh.

HELMER *comes out of his room, hat in hand, with his over-coat on his arm.*

(*Going toward him.*) Well, Torvald, dear, have you got rid of him?

HELMER. Yes; he's just gone.

NORA. May I introduce you?—This is Christina, who has come to town——

HELMER. Christina? Pardon me, but I don't know——?

NORA. Mrs. Linden, Torvald dear—Christina Linden.

HELMER (*to* MRS. LINDEN). A school-friend of my wife's, no doubt?

MRS. LINDEN. Yes; we knew each other as girls.

NORA. And only think! She has taken this long journey on purpose to speak to you.

* "Död og pine," literally "death and torture;" but by usage a comparatively mild oath.

HELMER. To speak to me!

MRS. LINDEN. Well, not quite——

NORA. You see Christina is tremendously clever at accounts, and she is so anxious to work under a first-rate man of business in order to learn still more——

HELMER. Very sensible indeed.

NORA. And when she heard you were appointed Manager—it was telegraphed, you know—she started off at once, and—Torvald dear, for my sake, you must do something for Christina. Now can't you?

HELMER. It's not impossible. I presume you are a widow?

MRS. LINDEN. Yes.

HELMER. And have already had some experience in office-work?

MRS. LINDEN. A good deal.

HELMER. Well then, it is very likely I may find a place for you.

NORA (*clapping her hands*). There now! there now!

HELMER. You have come at a lucky moment, Mrs. Linden.

MRS. LINDEN. Oh! how can I thank you——?

HELMER (*smiling*). There's no occasion. (*Puts his overcoat on.*) But for the present you must excuse me.

RANK. Wait; I'll go with you (*fetches his fur coat from the hall and warms it at the fire*).

NORA. Don't be long, dear Torvald.

HELMER. Only an hour; not more.

NORA. Are you going too, Christina?

MRS. LINDEN (*putting on her walking things*). Yes; I must set about looking for lodgings.

HELMER. Then perhaps we can go together?

NORA (*helping her*). What a pity we haven't a spare room for you; but I'm afraid——

MRS. LINDEN. I shouldn't think of troubling you. Good-by, dear Nora, and thank you for all your kindness.

NORA. Good-by for a little while. Of course you\ come back this evening. And you too, Doctor Rank. What! if you're well enough? Of course you'll be well enough. Only wrap up warmly. (*They go out into the hall, talking. Outside on the stairs are heard children's voices.*) There they are! there they are! (*She runs to the door and opens it. The nurse* ANNA *enters with the children.*) Come in! come in! (*Bends down and kisses the children.*) Oh! my sweet darlings! Do you see them, Christina? Aren't they lovely?

RANK. Don't let's stand here chattering in the draught.

HELMER. Come, Mrs. Linden; only mothers can stand such a temperature. (DR. RANK, HELMER, *and* MRS. LINDEN *go down the stairs;* ANNA *enters the room with the children;* NORA *also, shutting the door.*)

NORA. How fresh and bright you look! And what red cheeks you have!—like apples and roses. (*The children talk low to her during the following.*) Have you had great fun? That's splendid. Oh, really! you've been giving Emmy and Bob a ride on your sledge!—Both at once, only think! Why you're quite a man, Ivar. Oh, give her to me a little, Anna. My sweet little dolly! (*Takes the smallest from the nurse and dances with her.*) Yes, yes; mother will dance with Bob too. What! did you have a game of snow-balls? Oh! I wish I'd been there. No; leave them, Anna; I'll take their things off. Oh, yes, let me do it; it's such fun. Go to the nursery;

you look frozen. You'll find some hot coffee on the stove. (*The nurse goes into the room on the left.* NORA *takes off the children's things, and throws them down any- where, while the children talk to each other and to her.*) Really! A big dog ran after you all the way home? But he didn't bite you? No; dogs don't bite dear little dolly children. Don't peep into those parcels, Ivar. What is it? Wouldn't you like to know? Oh, take care—it'll bite! What! shall we have a game? What shall we play at? Hide-and-seek? Yes, let's play hide- and-seek. Bob shall hide first. Am I to? Yes, let me hide first. (*She and the children play, with laughter and shouting, in the room and the adjacent one to the right. At last* NORA *hides under the table; the children come rushing in, look for her, but cannot find her, hear her half-choked laughter, rush to the table, lift up the cover, and see her. Loud shouts. She creeps out, as though to frighten them. Fresh shouts. Meanwhile there has been a knock at the door leading into the hall. No one has heard it. Now the door is half opened and* KROGSTAD *is seen. He waits a little; the game is renewed.*)

KROGSTAD. I beg your pardon, Mrs. Helmer——

NORA (*with a suppressed cry, turns round and half jumps up*). Ah! What do you want?

KROGSTAD. Excuse me; the outer door was ajar— somebody must have forgotten to shut it——

NORA (*standing up*). My husband is not at home, Mr. Krogstad.

KROGSTAD. I know it.

NORA. Then—what do you want here?

KROGSTAD. To say a few words to you.

NORA. To me? (*To the children, softly.*) Go in to

Everyone and Nora plays, leaves and Krogstad then comes back to talk to Nora.

A DOLL'S HOUSE.   55

Anna. What? No, the strange man won't hurt mamma. When he's gone we'll go on playing. (*She leads the children into the left-hand room, and shuts the door behind them. Uneasy, with suspense.*) It's with me you wish to speak?

Krogstad. Yes.

Nora. To-day? But it's not the first yet——

Krogstad. No ; to-day is Christmas Eve. It will depend upon yourself whether you have a merry Christmas.

Nora. What do you want? I certainly can't to-day——

Krogstad. Never mind that just now. It's about another matter. You have a minute to spare?

Nora. Oh, yes, I suppose so ; although——

Krogstad. Good. I was sitting in the restaurant opposite, and I saw your husband go down the street.

Nora. Well !

Krogstad. With a lady.

Nora. What then ?

Krogstad. May I ask if the lady was a Mrs. Linden ?

Nora. Yes.

Krogstad. Who has just come to town ?

Nora. Yes. To-day.

Krogstad. I believe she's an intimate friend of yours ?

Nora. Certainly. But I don't understand——

Krogstad. I used to know her too.

Nora. I know you did.

Krogstad. Ah! you know all about it. I thought as much. Now, frankly, is Mrs. Linden to have a place in the bank ?

Nora. How dare you catechise me in this way, Mr.

Krogstad, you, a subordinate of my husband's? But since you ask you shall know. Yes, Mrs. Linden is to be employed. And it's I who recommended her, Mr. Krogstad. Now you know.

KROGSTAD. Then my guess was right.

NORA (*walking up and down*). You see one has a little wee bit of influence. It doesn't follow because one's only a woman that-——· When one is in a subordinate position, Mr. Krogstad, one ought really to take care not to offend anybody who—h'm——

KROGSTAD. Who has influence?

NORA. Exactly!

KROGSTAD (*taking another tone*). Mrs. Helmer, will you have the kindness to employ your influence on my behalf?

NORA. What? How do you mean?

KROGSTAD. Will you be so good as to see that I retain my subordinate position in the bank?

NORA. What do you mean? Who wants to take it from you?

KROGSTAD. Oh, you needn't pretend ignorance. I can very well understand that it cannot be pleasant for your friend to meet me; and I can also understand now for whose sake I am to be hounded out.

NORA. But I assure you——

KROGSTAD. Come now, once for all : there is time yet, and I advise you to use your influence to prevent it.

NORA. But, Mr. Krogstad, I have absolutely no influence.

KROGSTAD. None? I thought you just said——

NORA. Of course not in that sense—I! How should I have such influence over my husband?

KROGSTAD. Oh! I know your husband from our college days. I don't think he's firmer than other husbands.

NORA. If you talk disrespectfully of my husband, I must request you to go.

KROGSTAD. You are bold, madam.

NORA. I am afraid of you no longer. When New Year's Day is over, I shall soon be out of the whole business.

KROGSTAD (*controlling himself*). Listen to me, Mrs. Helmer. If need be, I shall fight as though for my life to keep my little place in the bank.

NORA. Yes, so it seems.

KROGSTAD. It's not only for the money : that matters least to me. It's something else. Well, I'd better make a clean breast of it. Of course you know, like every one else, that some years ago I—got into trouble.

NORA. I think I've heard something of the sort.

KROGSTAD. The matter never came into court ; but from that moment all paths were barred to me. Then I took up the business you know about. I was obliged to grasp at something ; and I don't think I've been one of the worst. But now I must clear out of it all. My sons are growing up ; for their sake I must try to win back as much respectability as I can. This place in the bank was the first step, and now your husband wants to kick me off the ladder, back into the mire.

NORA. But I assure you, Mr. Krogstad, I haven't the power to help you.

KROGSTAD. You have not the will ; but I can compel you.

NORA. You won't tell my husband that I owe you money !

KROGSTAD. H'm ; suppose I were to ?

NORA. It would be shameful of you ! (*With tears in her voice.*) This secret which is my joy and my pride— that he should learn it in such an ugly, coarse way— and from you ! It would involve me in all sorts of unpleasantness.

KROGSTAD. Only unpleasantness ?

NORA (*hotly*). But just do it. It will be worst for you, for then my husband will see what a bad man you are, and then you certainly won't keep your place.

KROGSTAD. I asked if it was only domestic unpleasantness you feared ?

NORA. If my husband gets to know about it, he will of course pay you off at once, and then we'll have nothing more to do with you.

KROGSTAD (*stepping a pace nearer*). Listen, Mrs. Helmer. Either you have a weak memory, or you don't know much about business. I must make your position clearer to you.

NORA. How so ?

KROGSTAD. When your husband was ill, you came to me to borrow twelve hundred dollars.

NORA. I knew nobody else.

KROGSTAD. I promised to find you the money——

NORA. And you did find it.

KROGSTAD. I promised to find you the money under certain conditions. You were then so much taken up about your husband's illness, and so eager to have the money for your journey, that you probably did not give much thought to the details. Let me remind you of them. I promised to find you the amount in exchange for a note of hand which I drew up.

NORA. Yes, and I signed it.

KROGSTAD. Quite right. But then I added a few lines, making your father a security for the debt. Your father was to sign this.

NORA. Was to? He did sign it!

KROGSTAD. I had left the date blank. That is to say, your father was himself to date his signature. Do you recollect that?

NORA. Yes, I believe——

KROGSTAD. Then I gave you the paper to send to your father. Is not that so?

NORA. Yes.

KROGSTAD. And of course you did so at once? For within five or six days you brought me back the paper, signed by your father, and I gave you the money.

NORA. Well! Haven't I made my payments punctually?

KROGSTAD. Fairly—yes. But to return to the point. You were in great trouble at the time, Mrs. Helmer.

NORA. I was indeed!

KROGSTAD. Your father was very ill, I believe?

NORA. He was on his death-bed.

KROGSTAD. And died soon after?

NORA. Yes.

KROGSTAD. Tell me, Mrs. Helmer: do you happen to recollect the day of his death? The day of the month, I mean?

NORA. Father died on the 29th of September.

KROGSTAD. Quite correct. I have made inquiries, and here comes in the remarkable point—(*produces a paper*) which I cannot explain.

NORA. What remarkable point? I don't know——

KROGSTAD. The remarkable point, madam, that your father signed this paper three days after his death !

NORA. What ! I don't understand——

KROGSTAD. Your father died on the 29th of September. But look here, he has dated his signature October 2d ! Is not that remarkable, Mrs. Helmer ? (NORA *is silent.*) Can you explain it ? (NORA *continues silent.*) It is noteworthy too that the words " October 2d " and the year are not in your father's handwriting, but in one which I believe I know. Well, this may be explained ; your father may have forgotten to date his signature, and somebody may have added the date at random before the fact of his death was known. There is nothing wrong in that. Everything depends on the signature. Of course it is genuine, Mrs. Helmer ? It was really your father who with his own hand wrote his name here ?

NORA (*after a short silence throws her head back and looks defiantly at him*). No ; I wrote father's name there.

KROGSTAD. Ah ! Are you aware, madam, that that is a dangerous admission ?

NORA. Why ? You'll soon get your money.

KROGSTAD. May I ask you one more question ? Why did you not send the paper to your father ?

NORA. It was impossible. Father was ill. If I had asked him for his signature I should have had to tell him why I wanted the money ; but he was so ill I really could not tell him that my husband's life was in danger. It was impossible.

KROGSTAD. Then it would have been better to have given up your tour.

NORA. No, I couldn't do that ; my husband's life depended on that journey. I couldn't give it up.

KROGSTAD. And did you not consider that you were playing me false?

NORA. That was nothing to me. I didn't care in the least about you. I couldn't endure you for all the cruel difficulties you made, although you knew how ill my husband was.

KROGSTAD. Mrs. Helmer, you have evidently no clear idea what you have really done. But I can assure you it was nothing more and nothing worse that made me an outcast from society.

NORA. You! You want me to believe that you did a brave thing to save your wife's life?

KROGSTAD. The law takes no account of motives.

NORA. Then it must be a very bad law.

KROGSTAD. Bad or not, if I lay this document before a court of law you will be condemned according to law.

NORA. I don't believe that. Do you mean to tell me that a daughter has no right to spare her dying father anxiety?—that a wife has no right to save her husband's life? I don't know much about the law, but I'm sure that, somewhere or another, you will find that *that* is allowed. And you don't know that—you, a lawyer! You must be a bad one, Mr. Krogstad.

KROGSTAD. Possibly. But business—such business as ours—I do understand. You believe that? Very well; now do as you please. But this I may tell you, that if I'm flung into the gutter a second time, you shall keep me company. (*Bows and goes out through hall.*)

NORA (*stands awhile thinking, then throws her head back*). Never! He wants to frighten me. I'm not so foolish as that. (*Begins folding the children's clothes. Pauses.*) But——? No, it's impossible. I did it for love!

CHILDREN (*at the door, left*).   Mamma, the strange man is gone now.

NORA. Yes, yes, I know.   But don't tell any one about the strange man.   Do you hear?   Not even papa!

CHILDREN. No, mamma; and now will you play with us again?

NORA. No, no, not now.

CHILDREN. Oh, do, mamma; you know you promised.

NORA. Yes, but I can't just now.   Run to the nursery; I've so much to do.   Run along, run along, and be good, my darlings! (*She pushes them gently into the inner room, and closes the door behind them.   Sits on the sofa embroiders a few stitches, but soon pauses.*) No! (*Throws down work, rises, goes to the hall-door and calls out.*) Ellen, bring in the Christmas-tree! (*Goes to table, left, and opens the drawer; again pauses.*) No, it's quite impossible!

ELLEN (*with the Christmas-tree*).   Where shall I stand it, ma'am?

NORA. There, in the middle of the room.

ELLEN. Shall I bring in anything else?

NORA. No, thank you, I have all I want.

(ELLEN, *having put down the tree, goes out.*)

NORA (*busy dressing the tree*).   There must be a candle here, and flowers there.—The horrid man! Nonsense, nonsense! there's nothing in it.   The Christmas-tree shall be beautiful.   I will do everything to please you, Torvald; I'll sing and dance, and——

Enter HELMER *by the hall-door, with bundle of documents.*

NORA. Oh! you're back already?

HELMER. Yes.   Has anybody been here?

NORA. Here?   No.

HELMER. Curious! I saw Krogstad come out of the house.

NORA. Did you? Oh, yes, by the bye, he was here for a minute.

HELMER. Nora, I can see by your manner that he has been asking you to put in a good word for him.

NORA. Yes.

HELMER. And you were to do it as if of your own accord? You were to say nothing to me of his having been here! Didn't he suggest that too?

NORA. Yes, Torvald; but——

HELMER. Nora, Nora! and you could condescend to that! To speak to such a man, to make him a promise! And then to tell me an untruth about it!

NORA. An untruth!

HELMER. Didn't you say nobody had been here? (*Threatens with his finger.*) My little bird must never do that again? A song-bird must never sing false notes. (*Puts his arm round her.*) That's so, isn't it? Yes, I was sure of it. (*Lets her go.*) And now we'll say no more about it. (*Sits down before the fire.*) Oh, how cosy and quiet it is here. (*Glances into his documents.*)

NORA (*busy with the tree, after a short silence*). Torvald.

HELMER. Yes.

NORA. I'm looking forward so much to the Stenborgs' fancy ball the day after to-morrow.

HELMER. And I'm on tenterhooks to see what surprise you have in store for me.

NORA. Oh, it's too tiresome!

HELMER. What is?

NORA. I can't think of anything good. Everything seems so foolish and meaningless.

HELMER. Has little Nora made that discovery?

NORA (*behind his chair, with her arms on the back*). Are you very busy, Torvald?

HELMER. Well——

NORA. What sort of papers are those?

HELMER. Bank business.

NORA. Already?

HELMER. I got the retiring manager to let me make some changes in the staff, and so forth. This will occupy Christmas week. Everything will be straight by the New Year.

NORA. Then that's why that poor Krogstad——

HELMER. H'm.

NORA (*still leaning over the chair-back, and slowly stroking his hair*). If you hadn't been so very busy I should have asked you a great, great favor, Torvald.

HELMER. What can it be? Let's hear it.

NORA. Nobody has such exquisite taste as you. Now, I should so love to look well at the fancy ball. Torvald dear, couldn't you take me in hand, and settle what I'm to be, and arrange my costume for me?

HELMER. Aha! so my wilful little woman's at a loss, and making signals of distress.

NORA. Yes *please*, Torvald. I can't get on without you.

HELMER. Well, well, I'll think it over, and we'll soon hit upon something.

NORA. Oh, how good that is of you! (*Goes to the tree again; pause.*) How well the red flowers show. Tell me, was it anything so very dreadful this Krogstad got into trouble about?

HELMER. Forgery, that's all. Don't you know what that means?

Nora. Mayn't he have been driven to it by need?

Helmer. Yes, or like so many others, done it out of heedlessness. I'm not so hard-hearted as to condemn a man absolutely for a single fault.

Nora. No, surely not, Torvald.

Helmer. Many a man can retrieve his character if he owns his crime and takes the punishment.

Nora. Crime?

Helmer. But Krogstad didn't do that; he resorted to tricks and dodges, and it's that that has corrupted him.

Nora. Do you think that——?

Helmer. Just think how a man with that on his conscience must be always lying and canting and shamming. Think of the mask he must wear even toward his own wife and children. It's worst for the children, Nora!

Nora. Why?

Helmer. Because such a dust-cloud of lies poisons and contaminates the whole air of home. Every breath the children draw contains some germ of evil.

Nora (*closer behind him*). Are you sure of that!

Helmer. As a lawyer, my dear, I've seen it often enough. Nearly all cases of early corruption may be traced to lying mothers.

Nora. Why—mothers?

Helmer. It generally comes from the mother's side, but of course the father's influence may act in the same way. And this Krogstad has been poisoning his own children for years past by a life of lies and hypocrisy— that's why I call him morally ruined. (*Stretches out his hands toward her.*) So my sweet little Nora must promise not to plead his cause. Shake hands upon it. Come, come, what's this? Give me your hand. That's right.

5

Then it's a bargain. I assure you it would have been impossible for me to work with him. It gives me a positive sense of physical discomfort to come in contact with such people. (NORA *snatches her hand away, and moves to the other side of the Christmas-tree.*)

NORA. How warm it is here; and I have so much to do.

HELMER. Yes, and I must try to get some of these papers looked through before dinner; and I'll think over your costume, too. And perhaps I may even find something to hang in gilt paper on the Christmas-tree! (*Lays his hand on her head.*) My precious little song-bird. (*He goes into his room and shuts the door behind him.*)

NORA (*softly, after a pause*). It can't be—— It's impossible. It must be impossible!

ANNA (*at the door, left*). The little ones are begging so prettily to come to mamma.

NORA. No, no, don't let them come to me! Keep them with you, Anna.

ANNA. Very well, ma'am. (*Shuts the door.*)

NORA (*pale with terror*). Corrupt my children!—— Poison my home! (*Short pause. She raises her head.*) It's not true. It can never, never be true.

ACT II.

[*The same room. In the corner, beside the piano, stands the Christmas-tree, stripped, and the candles burnt out. NORA's walking things lie on the sofa. NORA discovered walking about restlessly. She stops by sofa, takes up cloak, then lays it down again.*]

NORA. There's somebody coming. (*Goes to hall door; listens.*) Nobody; nobody is likely to come to-day, Christmas Day; nor to-morrow either. But perhaps —— (*Opens the door and looks out.*) No, nothing in the letter box; quite empty. (*Comes forward.*) Stuff and nonsense! Of course he only meant to frighten me. There's no fear of any such thing. It's impossible! Why, I have three little children.

Enter ANNA, from the left with a large cardboard box.

ANNA. At last I've found the box with the fancy dress.
NORA. Thanks; put it down on the table.
ANNA (*does so*). But it is very much out of order.
NORA. Oh, I wish I could tear it into a hundred thousand pieces.
ANNA. Oh, no. It can easily be put to rights—just a little patience.
NORA. I'll go and get Mrs. Linden to help me.

ANNA. Going out again! In such weather as this! You'll catch cold, ma'am, and be ill.

NORA. Worse things might happen—— What are the children doing?

ANNA. They're playing with their Christmas presents, poor little dears; but——

NORA. Do they often ask for me?

ANNA. You see they've been so used to having their mamma with them.

NORA. Yes; but, Anna, in future I can't have them so much with me.

ANNA. Well, little children get used to anything.

NORA. Do you think they do? Do you believe they would forget their mother if she went quite away?

ANNA. Gracious me! Quite away?

NORA. Tell me, Anna—I've so often wondered about it —how could you bring yourself to give your child up to strangers?

ANNA. I had to when I came as nurse to my little Miss Nora.

NORA. But how could you make up your mind to it?

ANNA. When I had the chance of such a good place? A poor girl who's been in trouble must take what comes. That wicked man did nothing for me.

NORA. But your daughter must have forgotten you.

ANNA. Oh, no, ma'am, that she hasn't. She wrote to me both when she was confirmed and when she was married.

NORA (*embracing her*). Dear old Anna—you were a good mother to me when I was little.

ANNA. My poor little Nora had no mother but me.

NORA. And if my little ones had nobody else, I'm sure

you would—nonsense, nonsense! (*Opens the box.*) Go in to the children. Now I must——. To-morrow you shall see how beautiful I'll be.

ANNA. I'm sure there will be no one at the ball so beautiful as my Miss Nora. (*She goes into the room on the left.*)

NORA (*takes the costume out of the box, but soon throws it down again*). Oh, if I dared go out. If only nobody would come. If only nothing would happen here in the meantime. Rubbish; nobody will come. Only not to think. What a delicious muff! Beautiful gloves, beautiful gloves! Away with it all—away with it all! One, two, three, four, five, six—— (*With a scream.*) Ah, there they come—— (*Goes toward the door, then stands undecidedly.*)

MRS. LINDEN *enters from hall where she has taken off her things.*

NORA. Oh, it's you, Christina. Is nobody else there? How delightful of you to come.

MRS. LINDEN. I hear you called at my lodgings.

NORA. Yes, I was just passing. I do so want you to help me. Let us sit here on the sofa—so. To-morrow evening there's to be a fancy ball at Consul Stenborg's overhead, and Torvald wants me to appear as a Neapolitan fisher girl, and dance the tarantella; I learnt it at Capri.

MRS. LINDEN. I see—quite a performance!

NORA. Yes, Torvald wishes me to. Look, this is the costume. Torvald had it made for me in Italy; but now it is all so torn, I don't know——

MRS. LINDEN. Oh! we'll soon set that to rights. It's

only the trimming that's got loose here and there. Have you a needle and thread? Ah! here's the very thing.

NORA. Oh, how kind of you.

MRS. LINDEN. So you're to be in costume, to-morrow, Nora? I'll tell you what—I shall come in for a moment to see you in all your glory. But I've quite forgotten to thank you for the pleasant evening yesterday.

NORA (*rises and walks across room*). Oh! yesterday, it didn't seem so pleasant as usual. You should have come a little sooner, Christina. Torvald has certainly the art of making home bright and beautiful.

MRS. LINDEN. You, too, I should think, or you wouldn't be your father's daughter. But tell me—is Doctor Rank always so depressed as he was yesterday?

NORA. No; yesterday it was particularly striking. You see he has a terrible illness. He has spinal consumption, poor fellow. They say his father led a terrible life—kept mistresses and all sorts of things—so the son has been sickly from his childhood, you understand.

MRS. LINDEN (*lets her sewing fall into her lap*). Why, my darling Nora, how do you learn such things?

NORA (*walking*). Oh! when one has three children one has visits from women who know something of medicine—and they talk of this and that.

MRS. LINDEN (*goes on sewing—a short pause*). Does Doctor Rank come here every day?

NORA. Every day. He's been Torvald's friend from boyhood, and he's a good friend of mine too. Doctor Rank is quite one of the family.

MRS. LINDEN. But tell me—is he quite sincere? I mean, doesn't he like to say flattering things to people?

NORA. On the contrary. Why should you think so?

MRS. LINDEN. When you introduced us yesterday he declared he had often heard my name; but I noticed your husband had no notion who I was. How could Doctor Rank——?

NORA. Yes, he was quite right, Christina. You see, Torvald loves me so indescribably he wants to have me all to himself, as he says. When we were first married he was almost jealous if I even mentioned one of the people at home; so I naturally let it alone. But I often talk to Doctor Rank about the old times, for he likes to hear about them.

MRS. LINDEN. Listen to me, Nora! You're still a child in many ways. I am older than you, and have more experience. I'll tell you something: you ought to get clear of the whole affair with Doctor Rank.

NORA. What affair?

MRS. LINDEN. You were talking yesterday of a rich admirer who was to find you money——

NORA. Yes, one who never existed, worse luck. What then?

MRS. LINDEN. Has Doctor Rank money?

NORA. Yes, he has.

MRS. LINDEN. And nobody to provide for?

NORA. Nobody. But——?

MRS. LINDEN. And he comes here every day?

NORA. Yes, every day.

MRS. LINDEN. I should have thought he'd have had better taste.

NORA. I don't understand you.

MRS. LINDEN. Don't pretend, Nora. Do you suppose I don't guess who lent you the twelve hundred dollars?

NORA. Are you out of your senses? You think *that!* A friend who comes here every day! How painful that would be!

MRS. LINDEN. Then it really is not he?

NORA. No, I assure you. It never for a moment occurred to me. Besides, at that time he had nothing to lend; he came into his property afterward.

MRS. LINDEN. Well, I believe that was lucky for you, Nora dear.

NORA. No, really, it would never have struck me to ask Doctor Rank. But I'm certain that if I did——

MRS. LINDEN. But of course you never would?

NORA. Of course not. It's inconceivable that it should ever be necessary. But I'm quite sure that if I spoke to Doctor Rank——

MRS. LINDEN. Behind your husband's back?

NORA. I must get out of the other thing; that's behind his back too. I must get out of that.

MRS. LINDEN. Yes, yes, I told you so yesterday; but——

NORA (*walking up and down*). A man can manage these things much better than a woman.

MRS. LINDEN. One's own husband, yes.

NORA. Nonsense. (*Stands still.*) When everything is paid, one gets back the paper?

MRS. LINDEN. Of course.

NORA. And can tear it into a hundred thousand pieces, and burn it, the nasty, filthy thing!

MRS. LINDEN (*looks at her fixedly, lays down her work, and rises slowly*). Nora, you're hiding something from me.

NORA. Can you see that in my face?

Mrs. Linden. Something has happened since yesterday morning. Nora, what is it?

Nora (*going toward her*). Christina (*listens*)—Hush! There's Torvald coming home. Here, go into the nursery. Torvald cannot bear to see dressmaking. Let Anna help you.

Mrs. Linden (*gathers some of the things together*). Very well, but I shan't go away until you've told me all about it. (*She goes out to the left as* Helmer *enters from hall.*)

Nora (*runs to meet him*). Oh! how I've been longing for you to come, Torvald dear.

Helmer. Was the dressmaker here?

Nora. No, Christina. She is helping me with my costume. You'll see how well I shall look.

Helmer. Yes, wasn't that a lucky thought of mine?

Nora. Splendid. But isn't it good of me, too, to have given in to you?

Helmer (*takes her under the chin*). Good of you! To give in to your own husband? Well, well, you little madcap, I know you don't mean it. But I won't disturb you. I dare say you want to be "trying on."

Nora. And you're going to work, I suppose?

Helmer. Yes. (*Shows her bundle of papers.*) Look here. (*Goes toward his room.*) I've just come from the Bank.

Nora. Torvald.

Helmer (*stopping*). Yes?

Nora. If your little squirrel were to beg you for something so prettily——

Helmer. Well?

Nora. Would you do it?

Helmer. I must know first what it is.

NORA. The squirrel would jump about and play all sorts of tricks if you would only be nice and kind.

HELMER. Come, then, out with it.

NORA. Your lark would twitter from morning till night——

HELMER. Oh, that she does in any case.

NORA. I'll be an elf and dance in the moonlight for you, Torvald.

HELMER. Nora—you can't mean what you were hinting at this morning?

NORA (*coming nearer*). Yes, Torvald, I beg and implore you.

HELMER. Have you really the courage to begin that again?

NORA. Yes, yes; for my sake, you must let Krogstad keep his place in the bank.

HELMER. My dear Nora, it's his place I intend for Mrs. Linden.

NORA. Yes, that's so good of you. But instead of Krogstad, you could dismiss some other clerk.

HELMER. Why, this is incredible obstinacy! Because you thoughtlessly promised to put in a word for him, I am to——

NORA. It's not that, Torvald. It's for your own sake. This man writes for the most scurrilous newspapers; you said so yourself. He can do you such a lot of harm. I'm terribly afraid of him.

HELMER. Oh, I understand; it's old recollections that are frightening you.

NORA. What do you mean?

HELMER. Of course you're thinking of your father.

NORA. Yes, of course. Only think of the shameful

things wicked people used to write about father. I believe they'd have got him dismissed if you hadn't been sent to look into the thing and been kind to him and helped him.

HELMER. My dear Nora, between your father and me there is all the difference in the world. Your father was not altogether unimpeachable. I am ; and I hope to remain so.

NORA. Oh, no one knows what wicked men can hit upon. We could live so happily now, in our cosy, quiet home, you and I and the children, Torvald! That's why I beg and implore you——

HELMER. And it's just by pleading his cause that you make it impossible for me to keep him. It's already known at the bank that I intend to dismiss Krogstad. If it were now reported that the new manager let himself be turned round his wife's little finger—— *patriarchal*

NORA. What then?

HELMER. Oh, nothing! So long as a wilful woman can have her way I am to make myself the laughing-stock of everyone, and set people saying I am under petticoat government? Take my word for it, I should soon feel the consequences. And besides, there's one thing that makes Krogstad impossible for me to work with.

NORA. What thing?

HELMER. I could perhaps have overlooked his shady character at a pinch——

NORA. Yes, couldn't you, Torvald?

HELMER. And I hear he is good at his work. But the fact is, he was a college chum of mine—there was one of those rash friendships between us that one so often re-

pents of later. I don't mind confessing it—he calls me
by my Christian name ; * and he insists on doing it even
when others are present. He delights in putting on airs
of familiarity—Torvald here, Torvald there ! I assure
you it's most painful to me. He would make my position at the Bank perfectly unendurable.

NORA. Torvald, you're not serious ?

HELMER. No ? Why not ?

NORA. That's such a petty reason.

HELMER. What ! Petty ! Do you consider me petty ?

NORA. No, on the contrary, Torvald dear ; and that's
just why——

HELMER. Never mind, you call my motives petty ; then
I must be petty too. Petty ! Very well. Now we'll
put an end to this once for all. (*Goes to the door into
the hall and calls.*) Ellen !

NORA. What do you want ?

HELMER (*searching among his papers*). To settle the
thing. (ELLEN *enters.*) There, take this letter, give it
to a messenger. See that he takes it at once. The ad-
dress is on it. Here is the money.

ELLEN. Very well. (*Goes with the letter.*)

HELMER (*arranging papers*). There, Madame Obstinacy !

NORA (*breathless*). Torvald—what was in that letter ?

HELMER. Krogstad's dismissal.

NORA. Call it back again, Torvald ! There is still
time. Oh, Torvald, get it back again ! For my sake,
for your own, for the children's sake ! Do you hear,
Torvald ? Do it. You don't know what that letter may
bring upon us all.

* In the original : " We say ' thou ' to each other."

HELMER. Too late.

NORA. Yes, too late.

HELMER. My near Nora, I forgive your anxiety, though it's anything but flattering to me. Why should I be afraid of a blackguard scribbler's spite? But I forgive you all the same, for it's a proof of your great love for me. (*Takes her in his arms.*) That's how it should be, my own dear Nora. Let what will happen—when the time comes, I shall have strength and courage enough. You shall see, my shoulders are broad enough to bear the whole burden.

NORA (*terror-struck*). What do you mean by that?

HELMER. The whole burden, I say.

NORA (*firmly*). That you shall never, never do.

HELMER. Very well ; then we'll share it, Nora, as man and wife. (*Petting her.*) Are you satisfied now? Come, come, come, don't look like a scared dove. It is all nothing—fancy. Now you must play the tarantella through, and practice the tambourine. I shall sit in my inner room and shut both doors, so that I shall hear nothing. You can make as much noise as you please. (*Turns round in doorway.*) And when Rank comes, just tell him where I'm to be found. (*He nods to her and goes with his papers into his room, closing the door.*)

NORA (*bewildered with terror, stands as though rooted to the ground, and whispers*). He would do it. Yes, he would do it. He would do it, in spite of all the world. No, never that, never, never! Anything rather than that! Oh, for some way of escape! What to do! (*Hall bell rings.*) Anything rather than that—anything, anything! (NORA *draws her hands over her face, pulls herself together, goes to the door and opens it.* RANK *stands outside, hanging up his greatcoat. During the fol-lowing, it grows dark.*)

NORA. Good afternoon, Doctor Rank. I knew you by your ring. But you mustn't go to Torvald now. I believe he's busy.

RANK. And you?

NORA. Oh, you know very well I've always time for you.

RANK. Thank you. I shall avail myself of your kindness as long as I can!

NORA. What do you mean? As long as you can?

RANK. Yes. Does that frighten you?

NORA. I think it's an odd expression. Do you expect anything to happen?

RANK. Something I've long been prepared for; but I didn't think it would come so soon.

NORA (*seizing his arm*). What is it, Doctor Rank? You must tell me.

RANK (*sitting down by the stove*). I am running down hill. There's no help for it.

NORA (*draws a long breath of relief*). It's you?

RANK. Who else should it be? Why lie to one's self? I'm the most wretched of all my patients, Mrs. Helmer. I have been auditing my life-account—bankrupt! Before a month is over I shall lie rotting in the church-yard.

NORA. Oh! What an ugly way to talk!

RANK. The thing itself is so confoundedly ugly, you see. But the worst of it is, so many other ugly things have to be gone through first. There is one last investigation to be made, and when that is over I shall know exactly when the break-up will begin. There's one thing

I want to say to you. Helmer's delicate nature shrinks
so from all that is horrible; I will not have him in my
sick room.

NORA. But, Doctor Rank——

RANK. I won't have him, I say—not on any account!
I shall lock my door against him. As soon as I have as-
certained the worst, I shall send you my visiting card
with a black cross on it; and then you will know that
the horror has begun.

NORA. Why you're perfectly unreasonable to-day.
And I did so want you to be in a really good humor.

RANK. With death staring me in the face? And to
suffer thus for another's sin! Where's the justice of it?
And in every family you can see some such inexorable
retribution——

NORA (*stopping her ears*). Nonsense, nonsense; now
cheer up.

RANK. Well, after all, the whole thing's only worth
laughing at. My poor innocent spine must do penance
for my father's wild oats.

NORA (*at table, left*). I suppose he was too fond of as-
paragus and Strasbourg paté, wasn't he?

RANK. Yes; and truffles.

NORA. Yes, truffles, to be sure. And oysters, I believe?

RANK. Yes, oysters; oysters of course.

NORA. And then all the port and champagne. It's sad
all these good things should attack the spine.

RANK. Especially when the spine attacked never had
the good of them.

NORA. Yes, that's the worst of it.

RANK (*looks at her searchingly*). H'm——

NORA (*a moment later*).   Why did you smile?

RANK. No ; it was you that laughed.

NORA. No; it was you that smiled, Doctor Rank.

RANK (*standing up*). You're deeper than I thought.

NORA. I'm in such a crazy mood to-day.

RANK. So it seems.

NORA (*with her hands on his shoulders*). Dear, dear Doctor Rank, death shall not take you away from Torvald and me.

RANK. Oh, you'll easily get over the loss.   The absent are soon forgotten.

NORA (*looks at him anxiously*). Do you think so ?

RANK. People make fresh ties, and then——

NORA. Who make fresh ties?

RANK. You and Helmer will, when I'm gone.   You yourself are taking time by the forelock, it seems to me.   What was that Mrs. Linden doing here yesterday?

NORA. Oh !   You're surely not jealous of Christina ?

RANK. Yes, I am.   She will be my successor in this house.   When I'm gone, this woman will perhaps——

NORA. Hush !   Not so loud ; she is in there.

RANK. To-day as well?   You see!

NORA. Only to put my costume in order—how unreasonable you are !   (*Sits on sofa.*) Now do be good, Doctor Rank.   To-morrow you shall see how beautifully I dance ; and then you may fancy that I am doing it all to please you—and of course Torvald as well.   (*Takes various things out of box.*) Doctor Rank, sit here, and I'll show you something.

RANK (*sitting*). What is it?

NORA. Look here.   Look!

RANK. Silk stockings.

NORA. Flesh-colored. Aren't they lovely? Oh, it's so dark here now; but to-morrow— No, no, no, you must only look at the feet. Oh, well, I suppose you may look at the rest too.

RANK. H'm——

NORA. What are you looking so critical about? Do you think they won't fit me?

RANK. I can't possibly have any valid opinion on that point.

NORA (*looking at him a moment*). For shame! (*Hits him lightly on the ear with the stockings.*) Take that. (*Rolls them up again.*)

RANK. And what other wonders am I to see?

NORA. You shan't see any more, for you don't behave nicely. (*She hums a little and searches among the things.*)

RANK (*after a short silence*). When I sit here gossiping with you, I simply can't imagine what would have become of me if I had never entered this house.

NORA (*smiling*). Yes, I think you do feel at home with us.

RANK (*more softly—looking straight before him*). And now to have to leave it all——

NORA. Nonsense. You sha'n't leave us.

RANK (*in the same tone*). And not to be able to leave behind the slightest token of gratitude; scarcely even a passing regret—nothing but an empty place, that can be filled by the first comer.

NORA. And if I were to ask for——? No——

RANK. For what?

NORA. For a great proof of your friendship.

RANK. Yes?— Yes?

6

NORA. No, I mean—for a very, very great service.

RANK. Would you really for once make me so happy?

NORA. Oh! you don't know what it is.

RANK. Then tell me.

NORA. No, I really can't; it's far, far too much—not only a service, but help and advice besides——

RANK. So much the better. I can't think what you can mean. But go on. Don't you trust me?

NORA. As I trust no one else. I know you are my best and truest friend. So I will tell you. Well, then, Doctor Rank, you must help me to prevent something. You know how deeply, how wonderfully Torvald loves me; he would not hesitate a moment to give his very life for my sake.

RANK (*bending toward her*). Nora, do you think he is the only one who——

NORA (*with a slight start*). Who——?

RANK. Who would gladly give his life for you?

NORA (*sadly*). Oh!

RANK. I have sworn that you shall know it before I—go. I should never find a better opportunity—— Yes, Nora, now you know it, and now you know too that you can trust me as you can no one else.

NORA (*standing up, simply and calmly*). Let me pass, please.

RANK (*makes way for her, but remains sitting*). Nora——

NORA (*in the doorway*). Ellen, bring the lamp. (*Crosses to the stove.*) Oh, dear, Doctor Rank, that was too bad of you.

RANK (*rising*). That I have loved you as deeply as—any one else? Was that too bad of me?

Nora. No, but that you should tell me so. It was so unnecessary——

Rank. What do you mean? Did you know——?

Ellen *enters with the lamp ; sets it on table and goes out again.*

Rank. Nora—Mrs. Helmer—I ask you, did you know?

Nora. Oh, how can I tell what I knew or didn't know. I really can't say—— How could you be so clumsy, Doctor Rank? It was all so nice!

Rank. Well, at any rate, you know now that I am yours, soul and body. And now, go on.

Nora (*looking at him*). Go on—now?

Rank. I beg you to tell what you want.

Nora. I can tell you nothing now.

Rank. Yes, yes! You mustn't punish me in that way. Let me do for you whatever a man can.

Nora. You can really do nothing for me now. Besides, I really want no help. You'll see it was only my fancy. Yes, it must be so. Of course! (*Sits in the rocking-chair smiling at him.*) You're a nice one, Doctor Rank. Aren't you ashamed of yourself now the lamp's on the table?

Rank. No, not exactly. But perhaps I ought to go ——for ever.

Nora. No, indeed you mustn't. Of course you must come and go as you've always done. You know very well that Torvald can't do without you.

Rank. Yes, but you?

Nora. Oh, you know I always like to have you here.

Rank. That's just what led me astray. You're a riddle to me. It has often seemed to me as if you liked being with me almost as much as being with Helmer.

NORA. Yes, don't you see?—there are some people one loves, and others one likes to talk to.

RANK. Yes—there's something in that.

NORA. When I was a girl I naturally loved papa best. But it always delighted me to steal into the servants' room. In the first place they never lectured me, and in the second it was such fun to hear them talk.

RANK. Oh, I see ; then it's their place I have taken ?

NORA (*jumps up and hurries toward him*). Oh, my dear Doctor Rank, I don't mean that. But you understand, with Torvald it's the same as with papa——

ELLEN *enters from the hall.*

ELLEN. Please, ma'am——(*Whispers to* NORA *and gives her a card.*)

NORA (*glances at the card*). Ah! (*Puts it in her pocket.*)

RANK. Anything wrong ?

NORA. No, not in the least. It's only—it's my new costume——

RANK. Why, it's there.

NORA. Oh, that one, yes. But it's another that——I ordered it——Torvald mustn't know——

RANK. Aha ! so that's the great secret.

NORA. Yes, of course. Do just go to him ; he's in the inner room ; do keep him as long as you can.

RANK. Make yourself easy ; he sha'n't escape. (*Goes into* HELMER'S *room.*)

NORA (*to* ELLEN). Is he waiting in the kitchen ?

ELLEN. Yes, he came up the back stair——

NORA. Didn't you tell him I was engaged?

ELLEN. Yes, but it was no use.

NORA. He won't go away?

ELLEN. No, ma'am, not until he has spoken with you.

NORA. Then let him come in; but quietly. And, Ellen——say nothing about it; it's a surprise for my husband.

ELLEN. Oh, yes, ma'am, I understand—— (*She goes out.*)

NORA. It's coming. It's coming after all. No, no, no, it can never be; it shall not! (*She goes to* HELMER's door and slips the bolt. ELLEN *opens the hall-door for* KROGSTAD, *and shuts it after him. He wears a travelling coat, high boots, and a fur cap.*)

NORA. Speak quietly; my husband is at home.

KROGSTAD. All right. I don't care.

NORA. What do you want.

KROGSTAD. A little information.

NORA. Be quick, then. What is it?

KROGSTAD. You know I've got my dismissal.

NORA. I could not prevent it, Mr. Krogstad. I fought for you to the last, but it was no good.

KROGSTAD. Does your husband care for you so little? He knows what I can bring upon you, and yet he dares——

NORA. How can you think I should tell him?

KROGSTAD. I knew very well you hadn't. It wasn't like my friend Torvald Helmer to show so much courage——

NORA. Mr. Krogstad, be good enough to speak respectfully of my husband.

KROGSTAD. Certainly, with all due respect. But since

you're so anxious to keep the matter secret, I suppose you're a little clearer than yesterday as to what you have done.

NORA. Clearer than you could ever make me.

KROGSTAD. Yes, such a bad lawyer as I——

NORA. What is it you want?

KROGSTAD. Only to see how you're getting on, Mrs. Helmer. I've been thinking about you all day. A mere money-lender, a penny-a-liner, a——in short, a creature like me——has a little bit of what people call "heart."

NORA. Then show it ; think of my little children.

KROGSTAD. Did you and your husband think of mine? But enough of that. I only wanted to tell you that you needn't take this matter too seriously. I sha'n't lodge any information for the present.

NORA. No, surely not. I knew you would not.

KROGSTAD. The whole thing can be settled quite quietly. Nobody need know. It can remain among us three.

NORA. My husband must never know.

KROGSTAD. How can you prevent it? Can you pay off the debt?

NORA. No, not at once.

KROGSTAD. Or have you any means of raising the money in the next few days?

NORA. None that I will make use of.

KROGSTAD. And if you had it would be no good to you now. If you offered me ever so much ready money you should not get back your I O U.

NORA. Tell me what you want to do with it.

KROGSTAD. I only want to keep it, to have it in my possession. No outsider shall hear anything of it. So, if you've got any desperate scheme in your head——

Nora. What if I have?

Krogstad. If you should think of leaving your husband and children——

Nora. What if I do?

Krogstad. Or if you should think of——something worse——

Nora. How do you know that?

Krogstad. Put all that out of your head.

Nora. How did you know what I had in my mind?

Krogstad. Most of us think of *that* at first. I thought of it, too; but I had not the courage——

Nora (*voicelessly*). Nor I.

Krogstad (*relieved*). No one hasn't. You haven't the courage either, have you?

Nora. I haven't, I haven't.

Krogstad. Besides, it would be very silly—when the first storm is over—— I have a letter in my pocket for your husband——

Nora. Telling him everything?

Krogstad. Sparing you as much as possible.

Nora (*quickly*). He must never have that letter. Tear it up. I will get the money somehow.

Krogstad. Pardon me, Mrs. Helmer, but I believe I told you——

Nora. Oh, I'm not talking about the money I owe you. Tell me how much you demand from my husband—— I'll get it.

Krogstad. I demand no money from your husband.

Nora. What *do* you demand then?

Krogstad. I'll tell you. I want to regain my footing in the world. I want to rise; and your husband shall help me to do it. For the last eighteen months my record has been spotless ; I've been in bitter need all the time ; but I was content to fight my way up, step by step. Now, I've been thrust down, and I won't be satisfied with merely being allowed to sneak back again. I want to rise, I tell you. I must get into the bank again, in a higher position than before Your husband shall create a place on purpose for me——

NORA. He will never do that !

KROGSTAD. He will do it ; I know him—he won't dare to refuse ! And when I'm in, you'll soon see ! I shall be the manager's right hand. It won't be Torvald Helmer, but Nils Krogstad, that manages the Joint Stock Bank.

NORA. That will never be.

KROGSTAD. Perhaps you'll——?

NORA. *Now* I have the courage for it.

KROGSTAD. Oh, you don't frighten me. A sensitive, petted creature like you——

NORA. You shall see, you shall see !

KROGSTAD. Under the ice, perhaps? Down in the cold, black water? And next spring to come up again, ugly, hairless, unrecognizable——

NORA. You can't terrify me.

KROGSTAD. Nor you me. People don't do that sort of thing, Mrs. Helmer. And, after all, what good would it be ? I have your husband in my pocket all the same.

NORA. Afterward ? When I am no longer——

KROGSTAD. You forget, your reputation remains in my hands ! (NORA *stands speechless and looks at him.*) Well, now you are prepared. Do nothing foolish. So soon as Helmer has received my letter I shall expect to hear from him. And remember that it is your husband himself who has forced me back again into such paths. That I will never forgive him. Good-by, Mrs. Helmer. (*Goes through hall. NORA hurries to the door, opens it a little, and listens.*)

NORA. He's going. He is not putting the letter into the box. No, no, it would be impossible. (*Opens the door farther and farther.*) What's that? He's standing still ; not going downstairs. Is he changing his mind? Is he——? (*A letter falls into the box. KROGSTAD'S footsteps are heard gradually receding down the stair. NORA utters suppressed shriek ; pause.*) In the letter-box. (*Slips shrinkingly up to the door.*) There it lies—— Torvald, Torvald—now we are lost !

MRS. LINDEN *enters from the left with the costume.*

MRS. LINDEN. There, I think it's all right now. Shall we just try it on ?

NORA (*hoarsely and softly*). Christina, come here.

MRS. LINDEN (*throws dress on sofa*). What's the matter? You look quite aghast.

NORA. Come here. Do you see that letter? There, see—through the glass of the letter-box.

MRS. LINDEN. Yes, yes, I see it.

NORA. That letter is from Krogstad——

MRS. LINDEN. Nora—it was Krogstad who lent you the money !

NORA. Yes, and now Torvald will know everything.

MRS. LINDEN. Believe me, Nora, it's the best thing for you both.

NORA. You don't know all yet. I have forged a name——

MRS. LINDEN. Good heavens !

NORA. Now listen to me, Christina, you shall bear me witness.

MRS. LINDEN. How "witness"? What am I to——?

NORA. If I should go out of my mind—it might easily happen——

MRS. LINDEN. Nora!

NORA. Or if anything else should happen to me—so that I couldn't be here myself——

MRS. LINDEN. Now, Nora, you're quite beside yourself!

NORA. In case any one wanted to take it all upon himself—the whole blame, you understand——

MRS. LINDEN. Yes, but how can you think——

NORA. You shall bear witness that it's not true, Christina. I'm not out of my mind at all; I know quite well what I'm saying; and I tell you nobody else knew anything about it; I did the whole thing, I myself. Don't forget that.

MRS. LINDEN. I won't forget. But I don't understand what you mean——

NORA. Oh, how should you? It's the miracle coming to pass.

MRS. LINDEN. The miracle?

NORA. Yes, the miracle. But it's so terrible, Christina;—it mustn't happen for anything in the world.

MRS. LINDEN. I will go straight to Krogstad and talk to him.

NORA. Don't; he will do you some harm.

MRS. LINDEN. Once he would have done anything for me.

NORA. He?

MRS. LINDEN. Where does he live?

Nora. Oh, how can I tell——? Yes; (*feels in her pocket*) here's his card. But the letter, the letter——!

Helmer (*knocking outside*). Nora.

Nora (*shrieks in terror*). What is it? What do you want?

Helmer. Don't be frightened, we're not coming in; you've bolted the door. Are you trying on your dress?

Nora. Yes, yes, I'm trying it on. It suits me so well, Torvald.

Mrs. Linden (*who has read the card*). Then he lives close by here?

Nora. Yes, but it's no use now. The letter is actually in the box.

Mrs. Linden. And your husband has the key?

Nora. Always.

Mrs. Linden. Krogstad must demand his letter back, unread. He must make some excuse——

Nora. But this is the very time when Torvald generally——

Mrs. Linden. Prevent him. Keep him occupied. I'll come back as quickly as I can. (*She goes out quickly through the hall door.*)

Nora (*opens Helmer's door and peeps in*). Torvald!

Helmer. Well, now may one come back into one's own room? Come, Rank, we'll have a look— (*In the doorway.*) But how's this?

Nora. What, Torvald dear?

Helmer. Rank led me to expect a grand dressing-up.

Rank (*in the doorway*). So I understood. I suppose I was mistaken.

Nora. No, no one shall see me in my glory till to-morrow evening.

HELMER. Why, Nora dear, you look so tired. Have you been practising too hard?

NORA. No, I haven't practised at all yet.

HELMER. But you'll have to——

NORA. Yes, it's absolutely necessary. But, Torvald, I can't get on without your help. I've forgotten everything.

HELMER. Oh, we'll soon freshen it up again.

NORA. Yes, do help me, Torvald. You must promise me.—Oh, I'm so nervous about it. Before so many people—this evening you must give yourself up entirely to me. You mustn't do a stroke of work! Now promise, Torvald dear!

HELMER. I promise. All this evening I will be your slave. Little helpless thing!—But, by the by, I must first—— (*Going to hall door.*)

NORA. What do you want there?

HELMER. Only to see if there are any letters.

NORA. No, no, don't do that, Torvald.

HELMER. Why not?

NORA. Torvald, I beg you not to. There are none there.

HELMER. Let me just see. (*Is going.* NORA, *at the piano, plays the first bars of the tarantella.*)

HELMER (*at the door, stops*). Aha!

NORA. I can't dance to-morrow if I don't rehearse with you first.

HELMER (*going to her*). Are you really so nervous, dear Nora?

NORA. Yes, dreadfully! Let me rehearse at once. We have time before dinner. Oh! do sit down and accompany me, Torvald dear; direct me as you used to do.

HELMER. With all the pleasure in life, if you wish it. *(Sits at piano. NORA snatches the tambourine out of the box, and hurriedly drapes herself in a long parti-colored shawl; then, with a bound, stands in the middle of the floor.)*

NORA. Now play for me! Now I'll dance! *(HELMER plays and NORA dances. RANK stands at the piano behind HELMER and looks on.)*

HELMER *(playing).* Slower! Slower!

NORA. Can't do it slower.

HELMER. Not so violently, Nora.

NORA. I must! I must!

HELMER *(stops).* Nora—that'll never do.

NORA *(laughs and swings her tambourine).* Didn't I tell you so?

RANK. Let me accompany her.

HELMER *(rising).* Yes, do—then I can direct her better. *(RANK sits down to the piano and plays. NORA dances more and more wildly. HELMER stands by the stove and addresses frequent corrections to her. She seems not to hear. Her hair breaks loose and falls over her shoulders. She does not notice it, but goes on dancing. MRS. LINDEN enters and stands spellbound in the doorway.)*

MRS. LINDEN. Ah!

NORA *(dancing).* We're having such fun here, Christina!

HELMER. Why, Nora dear, you're dancing as if it were a matter of life and death.

NORA. So it is.

HELMER. Rank, stop! this is the merest madness. Stop, I say! *(RANK stops playing, and NORA comes to a sudden standstill. HELMER going toward her.)* I couldn't have believed it. You've positively forgotten all I taught you.

NORA (*throws tambourine away*). You see for yourself.

HELMER. You really do want teaching.

NORA. Yes, you see how much I need it. You must practise with me up to the last moment. Will you promise me, Torvald?

HELMER. Certainly, certainly.

NORA. Neither to-day nor to-morrow must you think of anything but me. You mustn't open a single letter —mustn't look at the letter-box!

HELMER. Ah, you're still afraid of that man——

NORA. Oh, yes, yes, I am.

HELMER. Nora, I can see it in your face—there's a letter from him in the box.

NORA. I don't know, I believe so. But you're not to read anything now; nothing must come between us until all is over.

RANK (*softly to* HELMER). You mustn't contradict her.

HELMER (*putting his arm around her*). The child shall have her own way. But to-morrow night, when the dance is over——

NORA. Then you will be free.

ELLEN *appears in doorway, right.*

ELLEN. Dinner is ready, ma'am.

NORA. We'll have some champagne, Ellen!

ELLEN. Yes, ma'am. (*Goes out.*)

HELMER. Dear me! Quite a feast.

NORA. Yes, and we'll keep it up till morning. (*Calling out.*) And macaroons, Ellen—plenty—just this once.

HELMER (*seizing her hands*). Come, come, don't let's

have this wild excitement! Be my own little lark again.

NORA. Oh, yes I will. But now go into the dining-room ; and you too, Doctor Rank. Christina, you must help me to do up my hair.

RANK (*softly as they go*). There is nothing in the wind? Nothing—I mean——

HELMER. Oh, no, nothing of the kind. It's merely this babyish anxiety I was telling you about. (*They go out to the right.*)

NORA. Well ?

MRS. LINDEN. He's gone out of town.

NORA. I saw it in your face.

MRS. LINDEN. He comes back to-morrow evening. I left a note for him.

NORA. You shouldn't have done that. Things must take their course. After all, there's something glorious in waiting for the miracle.

MRS. LINDEN. What are you waiting for?

NORA. Oh, you can't understand. Go to them in the dining-room ; I'll come in a moment. (*MRS. LINDEN goes into dining-room ; NORA stands for a moment as though collecting her thoughts ; then looks at her watch.*) Five. Seven hours till midnight. Then twenty-four hours till the next midnight. Then the tarantella will be over. Twenty-four and seven? Still thirty-one hours to live.

HELMER *appears at door, right.*

HELMER. What's become of my little lark ?

NORA (*runs to him with open arms*). Here she is !

ACT III.

[*The same room. The table with the chairs around it is in the middle. A lamp lit on the table. The door to the hall stands open. Dance music is heard from the floor above. MRS. LINDEN sits by the table, and turns the pages of a book absently. She tries to read, but seems unable to fix her attention; she frequently listens and looks anxiously toward the hall door.*]

MRS. LINDEN (*looks at her watch*). Still not here; and the time's nearly up. If only he hasn't—— (*Listens again.*) Ah, there he is—— (*She goes into the hall and opens the outer door; soft footsteps are heard on the stairs; she whispers:*) Come in; there's no one here.

KROGSTAD (*in the doorway*). I found a note from you at my house. What does it mean?

MRS. LINDEN. I must speak with you.

KROGSTAD. Indeed? And in this house?

MRS. LINDEN. I could not see you at my rooms. They have no separate entrance. Come in; we are quite alone. The servants are asleep and the Helmers are at the ball upstairs.

KROGSTAD (*coming into room*). Ah! So the Helmers are dancing this evening. Really?

MRS. LINDEN. Yes. Why not?

KROGSTAD. Quite right. Why not?

MRS. LINDEN. And now let us talk a little.

KROGSTAD. Have we anything to say to each other?

MRS. LINDEN. A great deal.

KROGSTAD. I should not have thought so.

MRS. LINDEN. Because you have never really understood me.

KROGSTAD. What was there to understand? The most natural thing in the world—a heartless woman throws a man over when a better match offers.

MRS. LINDEN. Do you really think me so heartless? Do you think I broke with you lightly?

KROGSTAD. Did you not?

MRS. LINDEN. Do you really think so?

KROGSTAD. If not, why did you write me that letter?

MRS. LINDEN. Was it not best? Since I had to break with you, was it not right that I should try to put an end to your love for me?

KROGSTAD (*pressing his hands together*). So that was it? And all this—for the sake of money.

MRS. LINDEN. You ought not to forget that I had a helpless mother and two little brothers. We could not wait for you, as your prospects then stood.

KROGSTAD. Did that give you the right to discard me for another?

MRS. LINDEN. I don't know. I've often asked myself whether I did right.

KROGSTAD (*more softly*). When I had lost you the very ground seemed to sink from under my feet. Look at me now. I am a shipwrecked man clinging to a spar.

MRS. LINDEN. Rescue may be at hand.

KROGSTAD. It was at hand; but then you stood in the way.

7

Mrs. Linden. Without my knowledge, Nils. I did not know till to-day that it was you I was to replace in the bank.

Krogstad. Well, I take your word for it. But now you do know, do you mean to give way?

Mrs. Linden. No, for that would not help you.

Krogstad. Oh, help, help——! I should do it whether or no.

Mrs. Linden. I have learnt prudence. Life and bitter necessity have schooled me.

Krogstad. And life has taught me not to trust fine speeches.

Mrs. Linden. Then life has taught you a very sensible thing. But deeds you will trust?

Krogstad. What do you mean?

Mrs. Linden. You said you were a shipwrecked man, clinging to a spar.

Krogstad. I have good reason to say so.

Mrs. Linden. I am a shipwrecked woman clinging to a spar. I have no one to care for.

Krogstad. You made your own choice.

Mrs. Linden. I had no choice.

Krogstad. Well, what then?

Mrs. Linden. How if we two shipwrecked people could join hands?

Krogstad. What!

Mrs. Linden. Suppose we lashed the spars together?

Krogstad. Christina!

Mrs. Linden. What do you think brought me to town?

Krogstad. Had you any thought of me?

Mrs. Linden. I must have work, or I can't live. All

my life, as long as I can remember, I have worked ; work
has been my one great joy. Now I stand quite alone in
the world, so terribly aimless and forsaken. There is
no happiness in working for one's self. Nils, give me
somebody and something to work for.

KROGSTAD. No, no, that can never be. It's simply a
woman's romantic notion of self-sacrifice.

MRS. LINDEN. Have you ever found me romantic?

KROGSTAD. Would you really——? Tell me, do you
know my past?

MRS. LINDEN. Yes.

KROGSTAD. And do you know what people say of
me?

MRS. LINDEN. Did not you say just now that with me
you would have been another man?

KROGSTAD. I am sure of it.

MRS. LINDEN. Is it too late?

KROGSTAD. Christina, do you know what you are doing? Yes, you do ; I see it in your face. Have you the
courage?

MRS. LINDEN. I need some one to tend, and your children need a mother. You need me, and I—I need you.
Nils, I believe in your better self. With you I fear
nothing.

KROGSTAD (*seizing her hands*). Thank you—thank you,
Christina. Now I shall make others see me as you do.
Ah, I forgot——

MRS. LINDEN (*listening*). Hush! The tarantella! Go,
go !

KROGSTAD. Why? What is it?

MRS. LINDEN. Don't you hear the dancing overhead?
As soon as that is over they will be here.

KROGSTAD. Oh, yes, I'll go. But it's too late now. Of course you don't know the step I have taken against the Helmers ?

MRS. LINDEN. Yes, Nils, I do know.

KROGSTAD. And yet you have the courage to——

MRS. LINDEN. I know what lengths despair can drive a man to.

KROGSTAD. Oh, if I could only undo it !

MRS. LINDEN. You can——. Your letter is still in the box.

KROGSTAD. Are you sure ?

MRS. LINDEN. Yes, but——

KROGSTAD (*looking at her searchingly*). Ah, now I understand. You want to save your friend at any price. Say it out—is that your idea ?

MRS. LINDEN. Nils, a woman who has once sold herself for the sake of others does not do so again.

KROGSTAD. I will demand my letter back again.

MRS. LINDEN. No, no.

KROGSTAD. Yes, of course ; I'll wait till Helmer comes ; I'll tell him to give it back to me—that it's only about my dismissal—that I don't want it read.

MRS. LINDEN. No, Nils, you must not recall the letter.

KROGSTAD. But tell me, wasn't that just why you got me to come here ?

MRS. LINDEN. Yes, in my first terror. But a day has passed since then, and in that day I have seen incredible things in this house. Helmer must know everything ; there must be an end to this unhappy secret. These two must come to a full understanding. They can't possibly go on with all these shifts and concealments.

KROGSTAD. Very well, if you like to risk it. But one thing I can do, and at once——.

MRS. LINDEN (*listening*). Make haste. Go, go ! The dance is over ; we are not safe another moment.

KROGSTAD. I'll wait for you in the street.

MRS. LINDEN. Yes, do ; you must take me home.

KROGSTAD. I never was so happy in all my life ! (KROGSTAD *goes, by the outer door. The door between the room and hall remains open.*)

MRS. LINDEN (*setting furniture straight and getting her out-door things together*). What a change ! What a change ! To have some one to work for ; a home to make happy. I shall have to set to work in earnest. I wish they would come. (*Listens.*) Ah, here they are ! I must get my things on. (*Takes bonnet and cloak. HELMER's and NORA's voices are heard outside ; a key is turned in the lock, and HELMER drags NORA almost by force into the hall. She wears the Italian costume with a large black shawl over it. He is in evening dress and wears a black domino.*)

NORA (*still struggling with him in the doorway*). No, no, no ; I won't go in ! I want to go up-stairs again ; I don't want to leave so early !

HELMER. But, my dearest girl——!

NORA. Oh, please, please, Torvald, only one hour more.

HELMER. Not one minute more, Nora dear ; you know what we agreed ! Come, come in ; you are catching cold here ! (*He leads her gently into the room in spite of her resistance.*)

MRS. LINDEN. Good evening.

NORA. Christina !

HELMER. What, Mrs. Linden, you here so late!

MRS. LINDEN. Yes, pardon me! I did so want to see Nora in her costume!

NORA. Have you been sitting here waiting for me?

MRS. LINDEN. Yes, unfortunately I came too late. You had already gone up-stairs, and I couldn't go away without seeing you.

HELMER (*taking* NORA's *shawl off.*) Well then, just look at her! I think she's worth looking at. Isn't she lovely, Mrs. Linden?

MRS. LINDEN. Yes, I must say——

HELMER. Isn't she exquisite? Everyone said so. But she is dreadfully obstinate, dear little creature. What's to be done with her? Just think, I had almost to force her away.

NORA. Oh, Torvald, you'll be sorry some day you didn't let me stop, if only for one half hour.

HELMER. There! You hear her, Mrs. Linden? She dances her tarantella with wild applause, and well she deserved it, I must say—though there was, perhaps, a little too much nature in her rendering of the idea—more than was, strictly speaking, artistic. But never mind—she made a great success, and that's the main thing. Ought I to let her stop after that—to weaken the impression? Not if I know it. I took my sweet little Capri girl—my capricious little Capri girl, I might say—under my arm; a rapid turn round the room, a courtesy to all sides, and—as they say in novels—the lovely apparition vanished! An exit should always be effective, Mrs. Linden; but I can't get Nora to see it. By Jove, it's warm here. (*Throws his domino on a chair, and opens the door to his room.*) What! No light here? Oh, of course! Excuse me—— (*Goes in and lights candles.*).

Nora (*whispers breathlessly*). Well?

Mrs. Linden (*softly*). I have spoken to him.

Nora. And——?

Mrs. Linden. Nora—you must tell your husband everything——

Nora (*almost voiceless*). I knew it!

Mrs. Linden. You have nothing to fear from Krogstad; but you must speak out.

Nora. I shall not speak!

Mrs. Linden. Then the letter will.

Nora. Thank you, Christina. Now I know what I have to do. Hush!

Helmer (*coming back*). Well, Mrs. Linden, have you admired her?

Mrs. Linden. Yes; and now I'll say good-night.

Helmer. What, already? Does this knitting belong to you?

Mrs. Linden (*takes it*). Yes, thanks; I was nearly forgetting it.

Helmer. Then you do knit?

Mrs. Linden. Yes.

Helmer. Do you know, you ought to embroider instead?

Mrs. Linden. Indeed! Why?

Helmer. Because it's so much prettier. Look now! You hold the embroidery in the left hand so, and then work the needle with the right hand, in a long, easy curve, don't you?

Mrs. Linden. Yes, I suppose so.

Helmer. But knitting is always ugly. Look now, your

arms close to your sides, and the needles going up and down—there's something Chinese about it.—They really gave us splendid champagne to-night.

MRS. LINDEN. Well, good-night, Nora, and don't be obstinate any more.

HELMER. Well said, Mrs. Linden!

MRS. LINDEN. Good-night, Mr. Helmer.

HELMER (*going with her to the door*). Good-night, good-night; I hope you'll get safely home. I should be glad to—but really you haven't far to go. Good-night, good-night! (*She goes;* HELMER *shuts the door after her and comes down again.*) At last we've got rid of her; she's an awful bore.

NORA. Aren't you very tired, Torvald?

HELMER. No, not in the least.

NORA. Nor sleepy?

HELMER. Not a bit. I feel particularly lively. But you? You do look tired and sleepy.

NORA. Yes, very tired. I shall soon sleep now.

HELMER. There, you see. I was right after all not to let you stop longer.

NORA. Oh, everything you do is right.

HELMER (*kissing her forehead*). Now my lark is speaking like a reasonable being. Did you notice how jolly Rank was this evening?

NORA. Was he? I had no chance of speaking to him.

HELMER. Nor I, much; but I haven't seen him in such good spirits for a long time. (*Looks at* NORA *a little, then comes nearer her.*) It's splendid to be back in our own home, to be quite alone together! Oh, you enchanting creature?

NORA. Don't look at me in that way, Torvald.

HELMER. I am not to look at my dearest treasure?—
at the loveliness that is mine, mine only, wholly and entirely mine?

NORA (*goes to the other side of the table*). You mustn't
say these things to me this evening.

HELMER (*following*). I see you have the tarantella still
in your blood—and that makes you all the more enticing.
Listen! the other people are going now. (*More softly.*)
Nora—soon the whole house will be still.

NORA. I hope so.

HELMER. Yes, don't you, Nora darling? When we're
among strangers do you know why I speak so little to
you, and keep so far away, and only steal a glance at
you now and then—do you know why I do it? Because
I am fancying that we love each other in secret, that I
am secretly betrothed to you, and that no one guesses
there is anything between us.

NORA. Yes, yes, yes. I know all your thoughts are
with me.

HELMER. And then, when we have to go, and I put the
shawl about your smooth, soft shoulders, and this glorious neck of yours, I imagine you are my bride, that our
marriage is just over, that I am bringing you for the
first time to my home, and that I am alone with you for
the first time, quite alone with you, in your quivering
loveliness. All this evening I was longing for you, and
you only. When I watched you swaying and whirling
in the tarantella—my blood boiled—I could endure it
no longer; and that's why I made you come home with
me so early.

NORA. Go now, Torvald. Go away from me. I won't
have all this.

HELMER. What do you mean? Ah! I see you're teasing me! Won't! won't! Am I not your husband? (*A knock at the outer door.*)

NORA (*starts*). Did you hear?

HELMER (*going toward the hall*). Who's there?

RANK (*outside*). It's I; may I come in a moment?

HELMER (*in a low tone, annoyed*). Oh! what can he want? (*Aloud.*) Wait a moment. (*Opens door.*) Come, it's nice of you to give us a look in.

RANK. I thought I heard your voice, and that put it into my head. (*Looks round.*) Ah! this dear old place! How cosy you two are here!

HELMER. You seemed to find it pleasant enough upstairs, too.

RANK. Exceedingly. Why not? Why shouldn't one get all one can out of the world? All one can for as long as one can. The wine was splendid——

HELMER. Especially the champagne.

RANK. Did you notice it? It's incredible the quantity I contrived to get down.

NORA. Torvald drank plenty of champagne too.

RANK. Did he?

NORA. Yes, and it always puts him in such spirits.

RANK. Well, why shouldn't one have a jolly evening after a well-spent day?

HELMER. Well spent! Well, I haven't much to boast of.

RANK (*slapping him on the shoulder*). But I have, don't you see?

NORA. I suppose you've been engaged in a scientific investigation, Doctor Rank?

RANK. Quite right.

HELMER. Bless me! Little Nora talking about scientific investigations!

NORA. Am I to congratulate you on the result?

RANK. By all means.

NORA. It was good then?

RANK. The best possible, both for doctor and patient —certainty.

NORA (*quickly and searchingly*). Certainty?

RANK. Absolute certainty. Wasn't I right to enjoy myself after it?

NORA. Yes, quite right, Doctor Rank.

HELMER. And so say I, provided you don't have to pay for it to-morrow.

RANK. Well, in this life nothing's to be had for nothing.

NORA. Doctor Rank, aren't you very fond of masquerades?

RANK. Yes, when there are plenty of comical disguises.

NORA. Tell me, what shall we two be at our next masquerade?

HELMER. Little insatiable! Thinking of your next already!

RANK. We two? I'll tell you. You must go as a good fairy.

HELMER. Oh, but what costume would indicate that?

RANK. She has simply to wear her every-day dress.

HELMER. Capital! But don't you know what you yourself will be?

RANK. Yes, my dear friend, I'm perfectly clear upon that point.

HELMER. Well?

RANK. At the next masquerade I shall be invisible.

HELMER. What a comical idea !

RANK. There's a big, black hat—haven't you heard of the invisible hat? It comes down all over you, and then no one can see you.

HELMER (*with a suppressed smile*). No, you're right there.

RANK. But I'm quite forgetting what I came for. Helmer, give me a cigar, one of the dark Havanas.

HELMER. With the greatest pleasure. (*Hands case.*)

RANK (*takes one and cuts the end off*). Thanks.

NORA (*striking a wax match*). Let me give you a light.

RANK. A thousand thanks. (*She holds match. He lights his cigar at it.*) And now, good-by.

HELMER. Good-by, good-by, my dear fellow.

NORA. Sleep well, Doctor Rank.

RANK. Thanks for the wish.

NORA. Wish me the same.

RANK. You? Very well, since you ask me — sleep well. And thanks for the light. (*He nods to them both and goes out.*)

HELMER (*in an undertone*). He's been drinking a good deal.

NORA (*absently*). I dare say. (HELMER *takes his bunch of keys from his pocket and goes into the hall.*) Torvald, what are you doing there?

HELMER. I must empty the letter-box, it's quite full ; there will be no room for the newspapers to-morrow morning.

NORA. Are you going to work to-night?

HELMER. Not very likely ! Why, what's this? Some one's been at the lock.

NORA. The lock—— ?

HELMER. I'm sure of it. What does it mean? I can't think that the servants——? Here's a broken hairpin. Nora, it's one of yours.

NORA (*quickly*) It must have been the children.

HELMER. Then you must break them of such tricks. H'm, h'm! There! at last I've got it open. (*Takes contents out and calls into the kitchen.*) Ellen, Ellen, just put the hall-door lamp out. (*He returns with letters in his hand, and shuts the inner door.*) Just see how they've accumulated. (*Turning them over.*) Why, what's this?

NORA (*at the window*). The letter! Oh, no, no, Torvald!

HELMER. Two visiting cards—from Rank.

NORA. From Doctor Rank?

HELMER (*looking at them*). Doctor Rank. They were on the top. He must just have put them in.

NORA. Is there anything on them?

HELMER. There's a black cross over the name. Look at it. What a horrid idea! It looks just as if he were announcing his own death.

NORA. So he is.

HELMER. What! Do you know anything? Has he told you anything?

NORA. Yes. These cards mean that he has taken his last leave of us. He intends to shut himself up and die.

HELMER. Poor fellow! Of course I knew we couldn't hope to keep him long. But so soon—and then to go and creep into his lair like a wounded animal——

NORA. What must be, must be, and the fewer words the better. Don't you think so, Torvald?

HELMER (*walking up and down*). He had so grown into our lives. I can't realize that he's gone. He and his sufferings and his loneliness formed a sort of cloudy background to the sunshine of our happiness. Well, perhaps it's best so—at any rate for him. (*Stands still.*) And perhaps for us, too, Nora. Now we two are thrown entirely upon each other. (*Puts his arm round her.*) My darling wife! I feel as if I could never hold you close enough. Do you know, Nora, I often wish some danger might threaten you, that I might risk body and soul, and everything, everything, for your dear sake.

Nora (*tears herself from him and says firmly*). Now you shall read your letters, Torvald.

Helmer. No, no; not to-night. I want to be with you, sweet wife.

Nora. With the thought of your dying friend?

Helmer. You are right. This has shaken us both. Unloveliness has come between us—thoughts of death and decay. We must seek to cast them off. Till then we will remain apart.

Nora (*her arms round his neck*). Torvald! good-night, good-night.

Helmer (*kissing her forehead*). Good-night, my little bird. Sleep well, Nora. Now I'll go and read my letters. (*He goes into his room and shuts the door*).

Nora (*with wild eyes, gropes about her, seizes Helmer's domino, throws it round her, and whispers quickly, hoarse-ly, and brokenly*). Never to see him again. Never, never, never. (*Throws her shawl over her head.*) Never to see the children again. Never, never. Oh, that black icy water! Oh, that bottomless——If it were only over! Now he has it; he's reading it. Oh, no, no, no, not yet. Torvald, good-by. Good-by my little ones——! (*She is rushing out by the hall; at the same moment Hel-*

MER *tears his door open, and stands with an open letter in his hand.*)

HELMER. Nora !

NORA (*shrieking*). Ah—— !

HELMER. What is this ? Do you know what is in this letter.

NORA. Yes, I know. Let me go ! Let me pass !

HELMER (*holds her back*). Where do you want to go?

NORA (*tries to get free*). You sha'n't save me, Torvald.

HELMER (*falling back*). True ! Is it true what he writes ? No, no, it cannot be true.

NORA. It is true. I have loved you beyond all else in the world.

HELMER. Pshaw—no silly evasions.

NORA (*a step nearer him*). Torvald—— !

HELMER. Wretched woman ! what have you done ?

NORA. Let me go—you shall not save me. You shall not take my guilt upon yourself.

HELMER. I don't want any melodramatic airs. (*Locks the door*). Here you shall stay and give an account of yourself. Do you understand what you have done? Answer. Do you understand it ?

NORA (*looks at him fixedly, and says with a stiffening expression*). Yes ; now I begin fully to understand it.

HELMER (*walking up and down*). Oh, what an awful awakening ! During all these eight years—she who was my pride and my joy—a hypocrite, a liar—worse, worse —a criminal. Oh ! the hideousness of it ! Ugh ! Ugh ! (NORA *is silent, and continues to look fixedly at him.*) I ought to have foreseen something of the kind. All your father's dishonesty——be silent ! I say all your father's dishonesty you have inherited—no religion, no morality, no sense of duty. How I am punished for shielding him! I did it for your sake, and you reward me like this.

Nora. Yes—like this!

Helmer. You have destroyed my whole happiness. You have ruined my future. Oh! it's frightful to think of! I am in the power of a scoundrel; he can do whatever he pleases with me, demand whatever he chooses, and I must submit. And all this disaster is brought upon me by an unprincipled woman.

Nora. When I'm gone, you will be free.

Helmer. Oh, no fine phrases. Your father, too, was always ready with them. What good would it do to me if you were " gone," as you say? No good in the world! He can publish the story all the same; I might even be suspected of collusion. People will think I was at the bottom of it all and egged you on. And for all this I have you to thank—you whom I have done nothing but pet and spoil during our whole married life. Do you understand now what you have done to me?

Nora (*with cold calmness*). Yes.

Helmer. It's incredible. I can't grasp it. But we must come to an understanding. Take that shawl off. Take it off I say. I must try to pacify him in one way or other—the secret must be kept, cost what it may. As for ourselves, we must live as we have always done; but of course only in the eyes of the world. Of course you will continue to live here. But the children cannot be left in your care. I dare not trust them to you—— Oh, to have to say this to one I have loved so tenderly— whom I still——but that must be a thing of the past.

Henceforward there can be no question of happiness, but merely of saving the ruins, the shreds, the show of it ! (*A ring ;* HELMER *starts.*) What's that ? So late ! Can it be the worst ? Can he——? Hide yourself, Nora ; say you are ill. (NORA *stands motionless.* HEL-MER *goes to the door and opens it.*)

ELLEN (*half dressed, in the hall*). Here is a letter for you, ma'am.

HELMER. Give it to me. (*Seizes letter and shuts the door.*) Yes, from him. You shall not have it. I shall read it.

NORA. Read it !

HELMER (*by the lamp*). I have hardly courage to. We may be lost, both you and I. Ah ! I must know. (*Tears the letter hastily open ; reads a few lines, looks at an enclosure ; a cry of joy.*) Nora. (NORA *looks interrogatively at him.*) Nora ! Oh ! I must read it again. Yes, yes, it is so. I am saved ! Nora, I am saved !

NORA. And I ?

HELMER. You too, of course ; we are both saved, both of us. Look here, he sends you back your promissory note. He writes that he regrets and apologizes—that a happy turn in his life—— Oh, what matter what he writes. We are are saved, Nora ! No one can harm you. Oh ! Nora, Nora——; no, first to get rid of this hateful thing. I'll just see—— (*Glances at the I O U.*) No, I won't look at it ; the whole thing shall be nothing but a dream to me. (*Tears the I O U and both letters in pieces, throws them into the fire and watches them burn.*) There, it's gone. He wrote that ever since Christmas Eve—— Oh, Nora, they must have been three awful days for you !

8

Last

NORA. I have fought a hard fight for the last three days.

HELMER. And in your agony you saw no other outlet but——no ; we won't think of that horror. We will only rejoice and repeat—it's over, all over. Don't you hear, Nora? You don't seem to be able to grasp it. Yes, it's over. What is this set look on your face? Oh, my poor Nora, I understand ; you can't believe that I have forgiven you. But I have, Nora ; I swear it. I have forgiven everything. I know that what you did was all for love of me.

NORA. That's true.

HELMER. You loved me as a wife should love her husband. It was only the means you misjudged. But do you think I love you the less for your helplessness? No, no, only lean on me. I will counsel and guide you. I should be no true man if this very womanly helplessness did not make you doubly dear in my eyes. You mustn't think of the hard things I said in my first moment of terror, when the world seemed to be tumbling about my ears. I have forgiven you, Nora—I swear I have forgiven you.

NORA. I thank you for your forgiveness. (*Goes out, right.*)

HELMER. No, stay. (*Looks in.*) What are you going to do?

NORA (*inside*). To take off my doll's dress.

HELMER (*in doorway*). Yes, do, dear. Try to calm down, and recover your balance, my scared little song-bird. You may rest secure, I have broad wings to shield you. (*Walking up and down near the door.*) Oh, how lovely—how cosey our home is, Nora. Here you are safe; here I can shelter you like a hunted dove, whom I have saved from the claws of the hawk. I shall soon bring your poor beating heart to rest, believe me, Nora, I will. To-morrow all this will seem quite different—everything will be as before; I shall not need to tell you again that I forgive you; you will feel for yourself that it is true. How could I find it in my heart to drive you away, or even so much as to reproach you? Oh, you don't know a true man's heart, Nora. There is something indescribably sweet and soothing to a man in having forgiven his wife—honestly forgiven her from the bottom of his heart. She becomes his property in a double sense. She is as though born again; she has become, so to speak, at once his wife and his child. That is what you shall henceforth be to me, my bewildered, helpless darling. Don't worry about anything, Nora; only open your heart to me, and I will be both will and conscience to you. (*Nora enters, crossing to table in everyday dress.*) Why, what's this? Not gone to bed? You have changed your dress.

NORA. Yes, Torvald; now I have changed my dress.

HELMER. But why now so late?

NORA. I shall not sleep to-night.

HELMER. But, Nora dear——

NORA (*looking at her watch*). It's not so late yet. Sit down, Torvald, you and I have much to say to each other. (*She sits on one side of the table.*)

HELMER. Nora, what does this mean; your cold, set face——

NORA. Sit down. It will take some time; I have much to talk over with you. (*Helmer sits at the other side of the table.*)

HELMER. You alarm me ; I don't understand you.

NORA. No, that's just it. You don't understand me ; and I have never understood you—till to night. No, don't interrupt. Only listen to what I say. We must come to a final settlement. Torvald !

HELMER. How do you mean ?

NORA (*after a short silence*). Does not one thing strike you as we sit here ?

HELMER. What should strike me ?

NORA. We have been married eight years. Does it not strike you that this is the first time we two, you and I, man and wife, have talked together seriously ?

HELMER. Seriously ! Well, what do you call seriously ?

NORA. During eight whole years and more—ever since the day we first met—we have never exchanged one serious word about serious things.

HELMER. Was I always to trouble you with the cares you could not help me to bear ?

NORA. I am not talking of cares. I say that we have never yet set ourselves seriously to get to the bottom of anything.

HELMER. Why, my dear Nora, what have you to do with serious things ?

NORA. There we have it ! You have never understood me. I have had great injustice done me, Torvald. first by my father and then by you.

HELMER. What ! by your father and me ?—by us who have loved you more than all the world ?

NORA (*shaking her head*). You have never loved me. You only thought it amusing to be in love with me.

HELMER. Why, Nora, what a thing to say !

NORA. Yes, it is so, Torvald. While I was at home

with father he used to tell me all his opinions and I
held the same opinions. If I had others I concealed
them, because he would not have liked it. He used to
call me his doll child, and play with me as I played with
my dolls. Then I came to live in your house——

HELMER. What an expression to use about our marriage!

NORA (*undisturbed*). I mean I passed from father's
hands into yours. You settled everything according to
your taste; and I got the same tastes as you; or I pre-
tended to—I don't know which—both ways perhaps.
When I look back on it now, I seem to have been living
here like a beggar, from hand to mouth. I lived by
performing tricks for you, Torvald. But you would
have it so. You and father have done me a great
wrong. It's your fault that my life has been wasted.

HELMER. Why, Nora, how unreasonable and ungrate-
ful you are. Haven't you been happy here?

NORA. No, never; I thought I was, but I never was.

HELMER. Not—not happy?

NORA. No, only merry. And you have always been so
kind to me. But our house has been nothing but play-
room. Here I have been your doll-wife, just as at home
I used to be papa's doll-child. And the children in their
turn have been my dolls. I thought it fun when you
played with me, just as the children did when I played
with them. That has been our marriage, Torvald.

HELMER. There is some truth in what you say, exag-
gerated and overstrained though it be. But henceforth
it shall be different. Playtime is over; now comes the
time for education.

NORA. Whose education? Mine, or the children's.

HELMER. Both, my dear Nora.

NORA. Oh, Torvald, you can't teach me to be a fit wife for you.

HELMER. And you say that?

NORA. And I—am I fit to educate the children?

HELMER. Nora!

NORA. Did you not say yourself a few minutes ago you dared not trust them to me.

HELMER. In the excitement of the moment! Why should you dwell upon that?

NORA. No—you are perfectly right. That problem is beyond me. There's another to be solved first—I must try to educate myself. You are not the man to help me in that. I must set about it alone. And that is why I am now leaving you!

HELMER (*jumping up*). What—do you mean to say

NORA. I must stand quite alone to know myself and my surroundings; so I cannot stay with you.

HELMER. Nora! Nora!

NORA. I am going at once. Christina will take me in for to-night——

HELMER. You are mad. I shall not allow it. I forbid it.

NORA. It's no use your forbidding me anything now. I shall take with me what belongs to me. From you I will accept nothing, either now or afterward.

HELMER. What madness!

NORA. To-morrow I shall go home.

HELMER. Home!

NORA. I mean to what was my home. It will be easier for me to find some opening there.

HELMER. Oh, in your blind experience——

NORA. I must try to gain experience, Torvald.

HELMER. To forsake your home, your husband, and your children! You don't consider what the world will say.

NORA. I can pay no heed to that! I only know that I must do it.

HELMER. It's exasperating! Can you forsake your holiest duties in this way?

NORA. What do you call my holiest duties?

HELMER. Do you ask me that? Your duties to your husband and your children.

NORA. I have other duties equally sacred.

HELMER. Impossible! What duties do you mean?

NORA. My duties toward myself.

HELMER. Before all else you are a wife and a mother.

NORA. That I no longer believe. I think that before all else I am a human being, just as much as you are —or, at least, I will try to become one. I know that most people agree with you, Torvald, and that they say so in books. But henceforth I can't be satisfied with what most people say, and what is in books. I must think things out for myself and try to get clear about them.

HELMER. Are you not clear about your place in your own home? Have you not an infallible guide in questions like these? Have you not religion?

NORA. Oh, Torvald, I don't know properly what religion is.

HELMER. What do you mean?

NORA. I know nothing but what our clergyman told me when I was confirmed. He explained that religion was this and that. When I get away from here and stand alone I will look into that matter too. I will see whether what he taught me is true, or, at any rate, whether it is true for me.

HELMER. Oh, this is unheard of! But if religion cannot keep you right, let me appeal to your conscience —I suppose you have some moral feeling? Or, answer me, perhaps you have none?

NORA. Well, Torvald, it's not easy to say. I really don't know—I am all at sea about these things. I only know that I think quite differently from you about them. I hear, too, that the laws are different from what I thought; but I can't believe that they are right. It appears that a woman has no right to spare her dying father, or to save her husband's life. I don't believe that.

HELMER. You talk like a child. You don't understand the society in which you live.

NORA. No, I don't. But I shall try to. I must make up my mind which is right—society or I.

HELMER. Nora, you are ill, you are feverish. I almost think you are out of your senses.

NORA. I never felt so much clearness and certainty as to-night.

HELMER. You are clear and certain enough to forsake husband and children?

NORA. Yes, I am.

HELMER. Then there is only one explanation possible.

NORA. What is that?

HELMER. You no longer love me.

NORA. No, that is just it.

HELMER. Nora! Can you say so?

NORA. Oh, I'm so sorry, Torvald ; for you've always been so kind to me. But I can't help it. I do not love you any longer.

HELMER (*keeping his composure with difficulty*). Are you clear and certain on this point too ?

NORA. Yes, quite. That is why I won't stay here any longer.

HELMER. And can you also make clear to me, how I have forfeited your love ?

NORA. Yes, I can. It was this evening, when the miracle did not happen. For then I saw you were not the man I had taken you for.

HELMER. Explain yourself more clearly ; I don't understand.

NORA. I have waited so patiently all these eight years ; for, of course, I saw clearly enough that miracles do not happen every day. When this crushing blow threatened me, I said to myself, confidently, "Now comes the miracle !" When Krogstad's letter lay in the box, it never occurred to me that you would think of submitting to that man's conditions. I was convinced that you would say to him, "Make it known to all the world," and that then——

HELMER. Well ? When I had given my own wife's name up to disgrace and shame——?

NORA. Then I firmly believed that you would come forward, take everything upon yourself, and say, "I am the guilty one."

HELMER. Nora !

NORA. You mean I would never have accepted such a sacrifice? No, certainly not. But what would my assertions have been worth in opposition to yours?

That was the miracle that I hoped for and dreaded. And it was to hinder that that I wanted to die.

HELMER. I would gladly work for you day and night, Nora—bear sorrow and want for your sake—but no man sacrifices his honor, even for one he loves.

NORA. Millions of women have done so.

HELMER. Oh, you think and talk like a silly child.

NORA. Very likely. But you neither think nor talk like the man I can share my life with. When your terror was over—not for me, but for yourself—when there was nothing more to fear,—then it was to you as though nothing had happened. I was your lark again, your doll—whom you would take twice as much care of in the future, because she was so weak and fragile. (*Stands up.*) Torvald, in that moment it burst upon me, that I had been living here these eight years with a strange man, and had borne him three children——Oh! I can't bear to think of it—I could tear myself to pieces!

HELMER (*sadly*). I see it, I see it ; an abyss has opened between us——But, Nora, can it never be filled up?

NORA. As I now am, I am no wife for you.

HELMER. I have strength to become another man.

NORA. Perhaps—when your doll is taken away from you.

HELMER. To part—to part from you ! No, Nora, no ; I can't grasp the thought.

NORA (*going into room, right*). The more reason for the thing to happen. (*She comes back with out-door things and a small travelling bag, which she puts on a chair.*)

HELMER. Nora, Nora, not now ! Wait till to-morrow.

NORA (*putting on cloak*). I can't spend the night in a strange man's house.

HELMER. But can't we live here as brother and sister?

NORA (*fastening her hat*). You know very well that would not last long. Good-by, Torvald. No, I won't go to the children. I know they are in better hands than mine. As I now am, I can be nothing to them.

HELMER. But some time, Nora—some time——

NORA. How can I tell? I have no idea what will become of me.

HELMER. But you are my wife, now and always?

NORA. Listen, Torvald—when a wife leaves her husband's house, as I am doing, I have heard that in the eyes of the law he is free from all the duties toward her. At any rate I release you from all duties. You must not feel yourself bound any more than I shall. There must be perfect freedom on both sides. There, there is your ring back. Give me mine.

HELMER. That too?

NORA. That too.

HELMER. Here it is.

NORA. Very well. Now it is all over. Here are the keys. The servants know about everything in the house, better than I do. To-morrow, when I have started, Christina will come to pack up my things. I will have them sent after me.

HELMER. All over! All over! Nora, will you never think of me again?

NORA. Oh, I shall often think of you, and the children —and this house.

HELMER. May I write to you, Nora?

NORA. No, never. You must not.

HELMER. But I must send you——

NORA. Nothing, nothing.

HELMER. I must help you if you need it.

NORA. No, I say. I take nothing from strangers.

HELMER. Nora, can I never be more than a stranger to you?

NORA (*taking her travelling bag*). Oh, Torvald, then the miracle of miracles would have to happen.

HELMER. What is the miracle of miracles?

NORA. Both of us would have to change so that——Oh, Torvald, I no longer believe in miracles.

HELMER. But I will believe. We must so change that——?

NORA. That communion between us shall be a marriage. Good-by. (*She goes out.*)

HELMER (*sinks in a chair by the door with his face in his hands*). Nora! Nora! (*He looks around and stands up.*) Empty. She's gone! (*A hope inspires him.*) Ah! The miracle of miracles——?! (*Then below is heard the reverberation of a heavy door closing.*)

LaVergne, TN USA
21 March 2011
221017LV00005B/156/A